Week-by-Week Homework for Building Writing Skills

BY **MARY ROSE**

NEW YORK • TORONTO • LONDON • AUCKLAND • SYDNEY
MEXICO CITY • NEW DELHI • HONG KONG • BUENOS AIRES

Teaching
Resources

To Susan Baker, Margie Blake,

and Olita Heighton of Middleport, Ohio,

for being wonderful friends and

a great support group.

SPECIAL THANKS TO COLLEAGUES BARBARA DOERR, LISA RIDLEY, AND ANN SHELDON
OF LAKE SYBELIA ELEMENTARY SCHOOL, MAITLAND, FLORIDA,
AND TO TERRY COOPER AND MARIA L. CHANG OF SCHOLASTIC INC.

Editor: Maria L. Chang
Cover design by Maria Lilja
Interior design by Kathy Massaro

ISBN-13: 978-0-545-06407-1
ISBN-10: 0-545-06407-4
Copyright © 2009 by Mary Rose
All rights reserved.
Printed in the U.S.A.

4 5 6 7 8 9 10   40   15 14 13 12

Contents

Introduction

In 2002, I published *Week-by-Week Homework for Building Reading Comprehension & Fluency* for Grades 3–6. That was followed by two more versions of the same book, one for Grade 1 and one for Grades 2–3. These books have been so successful that I have decided to add another to the series: *Week-by-Week Homework for Building Writing Skills*. This book, along with *Week-by-Week Homework for Building Math Skills*, should provide you with enough homework assignments for an entire school year, as well as help you communicate with your students' parents in a very special way.

As parents read the weekly tips in these homework sheets, they will begin to understand what you are trying to accomplish in the classroom. They will have a better understanding of the writing process and how state writing assessments are scored. The format for *Week-by-Week Homework for Building Writing Skills* supports the writer in the classroom and does exactly what homework should do—provide follow-up practice at home. These pages provide parents with an explanation of the skill being studied, examples of students' work, and clear instructions for helping their child succeed. These assignments have proven to be very popular with the parents of my own fourth-grade students. I strongly suggest that you use this book in conjunction with my first book, *10 Easy Writing Lessons That Get Kids Ready for Writing Assessments*, which contains complete lessons for teaching the very skills on which this homework book is based.

Thank you for purchasing this book. I hope you find it helpful. If you have comments or questions, please contact me at **Marycath@aol.com** and be sure to visit my Web site, **Maryroseworkshops.com** to read a monthly teaching tip.

Mary Rose

National Writing Standards

The lessons and homework activities in this book meet these writing standards set by the International Reading Association and the National Council of Teachers of English:

❋ Students adjust their use of spoken, written, and visual language (e.g., conventions, style, vocabulary) to communicate effectively with a variety of audiences and for different purposes.

❋ Students employ a wide range of strategies as they write and use different writing process elements appropriately to communicate with different audiences for a variety of purposes.

❋ Students apply knowledge of language structure, language conventions (e.g., spelling and punctuation), media techniques, figurative language, and genre to create, critique, and discuss print and nonprint texts.

State Writing Standards

Most state assessments are scored holistically, which means that the reader/ scorer looks at the content and makes a judgment based on the total quality of the essay. Unlike analytic scoring, holistic scoring does not award points for the various elements of print. State assessments are usually scored on a scale of 1 to 4 (or to 6), with 4 (or 6) being the highest score.

State standards vary, of course, from state to state, if not in their intent, at least in their wording. The lessons and homework activities in this book meet the following standards, which have been compiled from several states. Each state uses some combination of these benchmarks to create a scoring rubric for student essays.

* The student prepares for writing by recording thoughts, focusing on a central idea and grouping related ideas, and identifying the purpose for writing.

* The essay should focus on a central topic (also called main idea, subject, purpose, prompt, or key event), have a logical organizational pattern, including a beginning, middle, and conclusion, and contain transitional devices.

* The essay should demonstrate a sense of wholeness.

* The essay should have variety in sentence structures.

* The essay should have complete sentences except when fragments are used purposefully.

* The essay should have development of specific details (also called supporting ideas or supporting details), including elaborations of description, concrete examples, or vignettes, to support a point.

* The essay should have the mark of the particular writer, also known as voice.

* The author should use figurative language effectively, including similes, metaphors, idioms, alliteration, hyperbole, and personification.

* Students should be able to write from different points of view.

* Description should paint a word picture for the reader.

* The essay should be inviting and easy to read.

* The essay should follow the conventions of print, including punctuation, capitalization, and spelling.

* The essay should demonstrate a command of language, including precision in word choice, subject/verb agreement, and correct verb and noun forms.

How to Use This Book

Here are some hints for success with this book:

1. Fill in the "due at school on" date before you make double-sided copies of the homework sheets.

2. Read the teacher text that goes with each lesson.

3. Conduct a mini-lesson based on that text.

4. Assist students in completing the front of each homework sheet.

5. Discuss the back of the homework sheet so students understand their assignment.

6. Try to complete all of the assignments in the section called "The Basics" first. After that, you can jump around in the lessons, as the assignments do not follow a specific order.

Other Ideas for Using This Book

* Remember that these assignments are just that: assignments. They are not intended to teach the skills that are featured on each page. You must teach the skills in your mini-lessons and when you are teaching "regular" writing of essays and stories. These homework assignments are considered practice and should not be sent home until you are sure students know and understand the concepts being presented.

* Do not expect the assignments in this book to prepare your students for state writing assessments. You still need to teach them to write complete expository and/or narrative essays. This book has simply broken down the skills into practice lessons for the students. (See my book *10 Easy Writing Lessons That Get Kids Ready for Writing Assessments* for suggestions on preparing students for state assessments.)

* You will notice that each note to the parent contains an example of the technique that is being taught in that lesson. Make sure that you complete the "We did this in class" side of the homework sheet during your mini-lesson. Doing so ensures that students know what to do when they get home and provides a sample for parents to follow. This also gives parents clear evidence of your teaching so they have a definite idea of what you are trying to accomplish with this lesson.

* Give students all week to return homework. Send it home on Monday and accept it on Tuesday, Wednesday, Thursday, or Friday. Make exceptions. I had one parent who worked nights through the week. I chose to accept her child's homework on Mondays so that she could help him complete it over the weekend.

* Three-hole punch each page before sending it home. Provide students with folders with fasteners in which to store all completed homework assignments. By the end of the school year, each student will have a collection of writing tips that will serve him or her well into the high school years. You may choose to send this folder home about once a month or once a grading period so that parents can see writing progress being made.

* Consider doing all of your mini-lessons on a big chart tablet. This is better than an overhead transparency because it can be permanently displayed in the classroom. It is better than the chalkboard, because it can be easily displayed for review purposes just before students write a complete essay.

Assessment Made Easy

Because parents will offer a wide range of assistance to their children, instead of carefully grading each paper for every detail, consider giving only full credit, partial credit, or no credit for these assignments. Skimming the answers will tell you if a student actually has acquired the skill you are working on. Indicate this in your grade book with a check, a check minus, or a zero. At the end of the grading period, use a homework grade to help you decide the student's letter grade in writing for the period. For example, if you gave eight homework assignments during the term, students who returned at least seven completed papers should receive an A; at least six, a B; five, a C; four, a D; and three or fewer, an F. I make the homework grade just one grade in a long line of marks for content and grammar on classroom essays.

If you need more justification for your grades, note the number of sentences or tasks the student had to complete, and score accordingly. I take off 10 points if the parent did not sign the homework. Return unsigned papers to the parent for a signature.

Subtract some credit each time a student does not begin a sentence or a proper name with a capital letter or omits ending punctuation. A student should not be given full credit if an otherwise perfect paper is lacking in these print conventions. These are the most basic elements of writing, and your students should have learned these by now.

Offer a second chance. Occasionally you will have a parent who did not understand the assignment and was unable to assist his or her child. Consider a phone call or a note to clarify things and give the student a second chance to get it right. The parents will love you for this—and remember: The goal of this project is to help the student become a better writer. If he totally missed the main message or misunderstood the skills presented, then he deserves a second chance to correct it. If all else fails, try to find a few minutes to assist the child yourself.

Dear Families,

We know that you are quite used to helping your child complete homework assignments; most teachers give reading and math assignments on a weekly basis. This year, however, will offer you a new challenge. Your child will be receiving writing homework each week. On the front of each homework sheet, you will find a note that explains the skill your child is working on, offers you an example of what your child is trying to learn, and gives you some hints for successful completion of the assignment. The activity in front of the sheet will have been completed in class, so that your child should know exactly what to do when he or she gets home.

Please read the note to the families and the example before helping your child with these weekly assignments. Then you are welcome to assist your child with the assignment on the back of the sheet. All of the actual writing should be done by the child. When finished, please sign the paper and return it to school by the date indicated at the bottom of the page.

Thank you in advance for your help with these assignments. If you have any questions concerning this project, please contact me. The first lesson is attached and is due back to school on Friday. Thank you for all your assistance in making your child be the very best student he or she can be!

Sincerely,

Your Child's Teacher

Section 1
The Basics

Dear Teachers,

Have you ever watched your students actually write a story? In the middle of their writing, if you ask them how the story ends, they usually say something like, "I don't know; I didn't write it yet!"

The first two lessons in this book are about planning an essay. Good writers plan their work and have some sort of an outline for where the story is going or what main ideas they intend to include. You can make the planning stage less painful if you make the graphic organizer very simple, use it over and over again, let students know they can make changes in the middle of their writing, and provide lots of modeling.

The planner featured in Writing Tips #1 and #2 is a very simple graphic organizer that can be used for any kind of writing. It shows students how to plan in the most basic way and encourages them to "write in a circle," which means that they include something from the introduction in their closing paragraph.

The organizer looks like a large plus sign. The planning begins in the upper left-hand corner, where students write the topic of the story or essay and a few details to get them started. Then they move to the upper right-hand corner, where they write either what happened first in the story or the first main topic of the expository essay. The next box is the lower right-hand corner, where students write what happened next or the second main topic. The box on the lower left-hand corner is for the story's ending or the third main topic. Since we want students to write in a circle, instead of having a separate box for the closing paragraph, we end up right back where we began—in the introductory box at the upper left-hand corner.

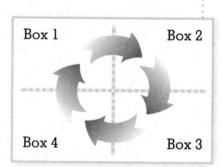

After planning their work, many students need help getting started. There are many ways to begin an essay, and this book teaches five. Next are some lessons on topic sentences and supporting details. The final lesson in this section teaches students how to write in a circle to create a whole and complete essay.

I hope you find these lessons helpful!

Mary

Make a plan before you begin to write an essay.

Start the lesson by asking students what they like about going to your school. Make a list of their reasons on the board, an overhead transparency, or chart paper. Try to get about 10 to 12 reasons. You may have to make suggestions, such as exciting field trips, a fun playground, or fabulous teachers!

Hand out copies of the homework sheet (page 19) and model how to complete Box 1 of the graphic organizer. After students have written the name of your school, the school mascot or motto, and other relevant information, have them refer back to the list and choose three reasons why your school is great. Each reason should go in a different box. You may also want to encourage students to write their own reasons, even if they are not on the list. Next, assist students in adding detail ideas. For example, if they like the new playground, they might describe the equipment out there.

"We did this in class" sample answers:

Topic: **What is good about our school?**

 Box 1

Name of school: *West Side School*

Mascot or motto: *Panther*

Principal: *Mr. Morris*

 Box 2

Write one reason this is a good school:

Great playground

Add two details about this reason:

Brand new

Good climbing equipment

Box 4

Write the third reason this is a good school:

Great teachers

Add two details about this reason:

Reasonable homework

Fun activities

Box 3

Write another reason this is a good school:

We have a strings music program.

Add two details about this reason:

We learn violin.

We have concerts for families.

After students have completed their graphic organizer, have them look over the homework for tonight. Discuss what they are supposed to do and the topic on which they are going to write. Remind them to have their parents sign their homework before returning it to school.

Writing Tip #2

Make a plan before you begin to write a story.

Ask students if anything exciting happened to them on their way to school today. Make a list of things they tell you. Then encourage them to think about what *could* have happened on their way to school. Try to elicit responses that are fictional, yet still reasonable. Add them to the list.

Hand out copies of the homework sheet (page 21). Invite students to choose a topic from the list or to think of their own topic. Assist them in completing the graphic organizer for a narrative story. It might help if you make your own graphic organizer on the board in front of the class. Make sure they can hear you "think out loud" as you write your ideas.

"We did this in class" sample answers:

Tip

The homework assignments in this book are designed to be used on a weekly basis. Please leave at least a week between Writing Tip #1 and Writing Tip #2. That should be just enough time to complete other writing lessons.

Topic: **Tell something exciting that happened on your way to school.**

Box 1

Where were you? *On the bus*

Who were you with?
Trevlin, Malcolm, Corey

Box 2

Tell what happened first.

Corey showed us his new GameBoy.

Write one or two details about what happened first.

We had to hide it because we are not supposed to bring those to school.

Box 4

Tell what happened third.

We got to school. Malcolm made Trevlin give it back.

Write one or two details about what happened third.

The GameBoy wasn't broken.

Box 3

Tell what happened second.

Malcolm was looking at the GameBoy, and he dropped it, and it slid across the aisle. Trevlin picked it up and said he was going to tell.

Write one or two details about what happened second.

Corey started crying. Trevlin was laughing.

When students have finished filling out their graphic organizers, invite volunteers to read their ideas out loud. Then discuss their homework assignment for tonight. Remind students that this is a personal narrative—they should write as if the events actually happened to them, even if they made the whole thing up. Remind them to have their parents sign their homework.

Note: Writing Tips #3 to #7 focus on five easy ways students can begin an essay. The directions for all five mini-lessons are the same: Explain to students that there are five good ways to start a story or an essay and that you will be exploring each of these ways one at a time. To simplify your mini-lessons, use the same prompt each time you introduce a new method: *If you could visit any place in the world, where would it be and why would you want to go there?*

Writing Tip #3

To start an essay, try using a question in the introduction.

Challenge students to brainstorm a list of questions they could use to start their essay. If they want, they could add a second and third sentence to support their opening question. Here are some sample questions:

* *Have you ever heard of a mouse named Mickey? My favorite place to visit is Disney World.*

* *Do you know what city is called the Big Apple? New York is the place where I would like to go.*

"We did this in class" sample answers:

Do you know the name of my favorite book? It is *Harry Potter and the Prisoner of Azkaban*. I could read this book over and over again.

What is that thing glistening on the sidewalk? On my way home yesterday, something shiny caught my eye. It was a diamond ring.

Writing Tip #4

To start an essay, try using a quotation in the introduction.

Invite students to brainstorm quotations that could be used with the writing prompt. Here are some suggestions:

* *"It's a small world after all!" Those famous words can be heard at my favorite place to visit. I love Disney World, and this essay will explain why it is so great.*

* *"If you can make it there, you can make it anywhere!" Where is there? New York City, of course. It is one of the most famous cities in the world and one of my favorite places to visit.*

"We did this in class" sample answers:

"Good morning, class!" That is what I hear every morning at 8:00. I would like to change the time that our school starts.

"Mom, I am sorry about that vase." Those words tell you that this story is going to be about a bad luck day.

Writing Tip #5

To start an essay, try using sound or motion words to set the mood.

Encourage students to brainstorm a list of sound or motion words that would be appropriate to use in an introduction. Here are some samples:

* *Bam! Boom! Pop! That's the sound of the wonderful fireworks that go off every night in my favorite place—Disney World. The fireworks are one reason that I love Disney World, and this essay will explain three other reasons this is a super place to visit.*

* *Slide! Shuffle! Slide! That's the sound of millions of passengers getting into the famous New York City subway. The subway is so exciting to me that it is one of the many reasons that New York is my favorite place in the world.*

"We did this in class" sample answers:

Rattle, rattle, toss! That's the sound of my family and me playing our favorite game, Monopoly. My dad and sister take this game seriously. But we always have fun!

Splash! Meow! I ran outside the door to see what happened. My cat had fallen into the pool! He was not happy at all.

NOTE: This lesson offers a great opportunity to introduce onomatopoeias. An onomatopoeia is a word that sounds like the sound it represents. For example, when you say the word *buzz*, you actually make a buzzing sound.

Writing Tip #6

To start an essay, sometimes you just need to start talking.

Explain to students that sometimes the best way to start an essay or a story is to simply start talking. Here are a few introductions that do just that:

* *My favorite place is Walt Disney World in Orlando, Florida. I love to go there to see all the exhibits, ride the rides, and watch the fireworks. I wish I could live at Disney World because it is so great.*

* *My favorite place is New York City. I love to look at the tall buildings, visit the museums, and ride the subway. There are millions of people who live there, so they must love it as much as I do.*

"We did this in class" sample answers:

I love to check my e-mail every day. It helps me stay in touch with my friends. That is one reason that computers are important to me.

My Aunt Carol is my favorite person in my family. She is my mom's younger sister. I love to visit her house and ride her horse, Lady Velvet.

Writing Tip #7

What if you can't think of a good introduction? If all else fails, restate the prompt.

This particular mini-lesson is designed for students who take state writing assessments and who get stuck during a test because they have no idea how to begin writing—even though they have just learned four ways to start an essay or story. Because state assessments are timed, it is important that students start writing quickly. They can do so by simply restating the prompt.

* *If I could go anywhere in the world, I would like to go to _____. This essay will explain why _____ is such a great place to visit.*

* *Most people have a favorite holiday or time of the year. My favorite holiday is _____ and this essay will tell you why I like it the best.*

"We did this in class" sample answers:

Almost everyone has a favorite day of the week. Friday is my favorite day. In this essay, I will explain why.

One day I was taking out the garbage. Then I saw a bright green light in the sky. You would never guess what happened next.

Writing Tip #8

Write a clear topic sentence and support it with details.

When students first begin to write pieces of substantial length, their topic sentence will almost always be the first sentence in the paragraph. For our purposes, students will tell either what they are going to explain (expository essay) or what happened in the story (narrative essay), and then follow that with details that further support their topic sentence.

For example, after writing an introduction about why a person is a child's best friend, a student might write this topic sentence:

Jade is my friend because she is always helpful to everyone.

That is clearly a topic sentence. The writer should then follow up by explaining what the sentence means:

Jade loans people books and helps everyone with homework. She is kind to everyone and helpful even to the teachers!

The sentences that follow the topic sentence are usually called supporting details or extensions, depending on the writing program you are using or the state in which you live.

If students are writing a narrative essay, a topic sentence might look something like this:

The troll was ugly!

This topic sentence needs an explanation:

It had long, black, greasy hair and a dirt-covered face. His teeth were green and slimy. He wore filthy torn clothes and was barefooted. He smelled like rotten eggs.

Hand out copies of the homework sheet (page 33). The assignment is twofold: It asks students to write a topic sentence for some supporting details and to write supporting details given a topic sentence.

"We did this in class" sample answers:

I loved running a race at our school field day.

You will not believe what is in my desk! It is crammed full of papers and notes that should have gone home to my mom. I have about 300 crayons and at least 20 markers. There is even a candy bar stuffed way in the back!

HINT: Notice that the topic sentences on page 16 are all quite short. Encourage students to write a short topic sentence. This allows them to put all of the interesting details in the supporting text.

As students become better writers, the topic sentence can move around the paragraph. Here's an example of a topic sentence at the end of the paragraph:

The troll had long, black, greasy hair and a dirt-covered face. His teeth were green and slimy. He wore filthy torn clothes and was barefooted. He smelled like rotten eggs. **He was ugly!**

Here's an example with the topic sentence in the middle of the paragraph:

The troll had long, black, greasy hair and a dirt-covered face. His teeth were green and slimy. He wore filthy torn clothes and was barefooted. **He was ugly!** *He smelled like rotten eggs.*

Writing Tip #9

Write a closing sentence for your paragraph.

Wouldn't it be wonderful if every paragraph your students wrote came with a topic sentence, supporting details, and a reasonable closing sentence? Sometimes students' closing sentences are contrived and artificial and detract from the overall quality of the essay.

Remind students that the closing sentence recaps the events of the story or summarizes the information. A really easy way to teach beginning writers to write a closing sentence is to have them simply say the same thing again, but with different words. Let's go back to the sample topic in Writing Tip #8:

Jade is my friend because she is always helpful to everyone. *Jade loans people books and helps everyone with homework. She is kind to everyone and helpful even to the teachers!* **It is nice to have such a wonderful friend.**

The closing sentence in this paragraph restates that Jade is a friend but in different words.

To help reinforce this lesson, make a transparency of the homework sheet (page 35) or write the practice activity on the board or chart paper. Use different colors of markers to write the topic and closing sentences. Be sure to point out that both sentences say the same thing and can often be interchanged.

"We did this in class" sample answers:

Topic sentence: We had a great time in art class today.

Closing sentence: We loved Mr. Catogni's art class today.

Last week we had the easiest assignment ever. **Miss Ridley asked us to come to the chalkboard and write our names on a piece of giant graph paper. We wrote names using the letters of other kids' names. It looked like a giant Scrabble board. When it was finished, we had to tell the class who we were named for or why we had this name.** I wish we had more easy assignments like this one!

Writing Tip #10

Write in a circle to make your piece feel whole and complete.

"Writing in a circle" means choosing an idea, name, phrase, or subject from the introduction and using it in the conclusion of an essay or story. Professional writers use this technique quite often, especially in short pieces such as magazine or newspaper articles.

When students are writing essays or stories, they tend to think that the final reason in an expository essay or the final event in a narrative is the closing. This activity will help them understand that the closing is a separate paragraph, just as the introduction is separate. The introduction is not what happened first, and the closing is not what happened last.

To help students actually see this, you might want to use colored markers as you model writing. Use one color for the introduction and closing, and a second color for the body of the piece. You can reinforce this even more if you have students circle the words that are the same in the introduction and closing. Hand out copies of the homework sheet (page 37) and complete the activity together with the class before sending it home.

"We did this in class" sample answers:

Now you know all of the reasons that I chose to write about my special friend, Donna. It is great to have a friendship that lasts so many years. I hope we will always be buddies and pals!

Well, that is the story of my bloody day in kindergarten. I will never forget that day when I was only five years old. I hope I don't bleed that much when I lose my next tooth!

Dear Families,

An important step in writing well is planning well. We strongly encourage students to make a plan before they begin writing. During this planning stage, your child is not required to actually write the essay yet.

Today's lesson focused on *expository* writing. An expository essay explains or gives information. All good essays need a strong beginning, a detailed middle part, and a definite closing. Notice that the graphic organizer below has only four sections: Box 1 introduces the topic, while Boxes 2, 3, and 4 contain the body of the essay—its main ideas and details. What about the closing? We will end right where we began, at the first box. Because we are using this format, the closing does not need a separate box.

The graphic organizer below was completed in class. This will help you understand how you and your child should complete the homework assignment on the back of this sheet.

Writing Tip #1

Make a plan before you begin to write an essay.

Your Child's Teacher,

_____

We did this in class!

Topic: **What is good about our school?**

Box 1

Name of school:

_____

Mascot or motto:

_____

Principal, address, or other important information:

_____

_____

Box 2

Write one reason this is a good school:

_____

Add two details about this reason:

_____

_____

Box 4

Write the third reason this is a good school:

_____

Add two details about this reason:

_____

_____

Box 3

Write another reason this is a good school:

_____

Add two details about this reason:

_____

_____

Families, please help!

Directions: Use the graphic organizer below to plan a simple, five-paragraph essay. After you answer the prompts, your responses in each box can easily be turned into a paragraph. The closing part of this essay is a separate, fifth paragraph that contains roughly the same information as the opening paragraph. While you will not always be using this simple form, it is a good place to start learning how to plan and write.

Topic: What do you like about living in our state?

Box 1

Name of state:

_____

State motto:

_____

Climate or location:

_____

Box 2

Write one reason you like living in this state:

_____

Add two details about this reason:

_____

_____

Box 4

Write the third reason you like living here:

_____

Add two details about this reason:

_____

_____

Box 3

Write another reason you like living here:

_____

Add two details about this reason:

_____

_____

❄ **This assignment is due at school on** _____ .

_____   _____
Child's name   Parent's signature

     Week-by-Week Homework for Building Writing Skills © 2009 by Mary Rose, Scholastic Inc.

Dear Families,

An important step in writing well is planning well. We strongly encourage students to make a plan before they begin writing. During this planning stage, your child is not required to actually write the story yet.

Today's lesson focused on *narrative* writing. A narrative essay tells a story. It starts with a strong and exciting introduction, followed by two to four events in the story, then a conclusion. The graphic organizer below is designed to help students plan their story. Since the closing will contain the same information as the introduction, it does not get a separate box. (Note that the conclusion is a separate paragraph and is not the last thing that happened in the story.)

Today in class we practiced making a plan for a story. Please read the example below carefully and follow it to complete this homework assignment.

Your Child's Teacher,

_____

We did this in class!

Writing Tip #2

Make a plan before you begin to write a story.

Topic: **Tell something exciting that happened on your way to school.**

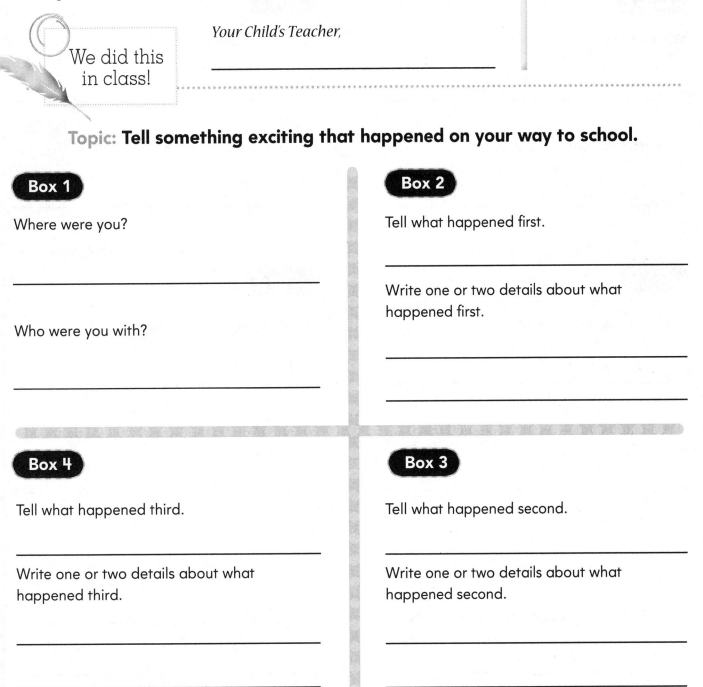

Box 1

Where were you?

_____

Who were you with?

_____

Box 2

Tell what happened first.

_____

Write one or two details about what happened first.

_____

_____

Box 4

Tell what happened third.

_____

Write one or two details about what happened third.

_____

_____

Box 3

Tell what happened second.

_____

Write one or two details about what happened second.

_____

_____

Families, please help!

Directions: Use the graphic organizer below to plan a simple, five-paragraph narrative essay. After you answer the prompts, your responses in each box can easily be turned into a paragraph. The closing part of this essay is a separate, fifth paragraph that contains roughly the same information as the opening paragraph. While you will not always be using this simple form, it is a good place to start learning how to plan and write.

Topic: **Tell a story about what happened after school one day.**

(NOTE: This can be fictional.)

Box 1

Where were you?

_____

Who were you with?

_____

Box 2

Tell what happened first.

_____

Write a detail about what happened first.

_____

Box 4

Tell what happened third.

_____

Write a detail about what happened third.

_____

Box 3

Tell what happened second.

_____

Write a detail about what happened second.

_____

✳ **This assignment is due at school on** _____ .

_____   _____
Child's name   Parent's signature

Week-by-Week Homework for Building Writing Skills © 2009 by Mary Rose, Scholastic Inc.

Dear Families,

Did you know that an introduction has two purposes? An introduction tells the reader what the passage is going to be about and makes him or her want to read it. That's why the introduction needs to be exciting and well written. There are many ways to begin an essay or story, but elementary school students need to learn only four or five. Today's lesson is about using a question in the introduction, whether for an expository or a narrative essay.

Please pay close attention to the practice your child completed in class, as it will help you with the rest of the assignment.

Your Child's Teacher, _____

To start an essay, try using a question in the introduction.

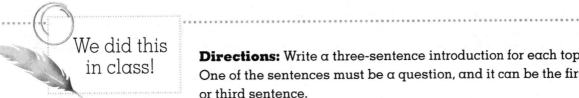

We did this in class!

Directions: Write a three-sentence introduction for each topic below. One of the sentences must be a question, and it can be the first, second, or third sentence.

1. **Explain why a particular book is your favorite.**

_____

_____

_____

_____

_____

_____

2. **Tell what happened when you found something exciting.**

_____

_____

_____

_____

_____

_____

Week-by-Week Homework for Building Writing Skills © 2009 by Mary Rose, Scholastic Inc.

Families, please help!

Directions: Can you think of a good way to begin an essay or story? One way is to ask a question. Write a three-sentence introduction for each topic below. One sentence must be a question, and it can be the first, second, or third sentence. Please note that your responses do not have to be real; they can be fiction.

1. **Explain what you would like to be when you grow up and why you chose that profession.**

_____

_____

_____

_____

_____

_____

2. **Tell a story about why you were late for school one day.**

_____

_____

_____

_____

_____

_____

✳ **This assignment is due at school on** _____ .

_____   _____
        Child's name   Parent's signature

Week-by-Week Homework for Building Writing Skills © 2009 by Mary Rose, Scholastic Inc.

Dear Families,

"Ready, set, go!" One easy way to begin an essay is to use a quotation. For this activity, your child needs only one sentence that is a direct quote of what someone has said. The introduction, however, should have at least three sentences, with the quote at the beginning, middle, or end. Here are some hints for using quotes in an introduction:

- The quote can be famous: "A penny saved is a penny earned." *Theme*
- It can be actual words someone has uttered: "Susan, please take these papers to the office," said Mrs. Sheldon.
- It can be a made-up quote from a real or fictional character: "Land, ho!" yelled Christopher Columbus. "Watch out for the dementors!" warned Harry Potter.

Your Child's Teacher, _____

Writing Tip #4

To start an essay, try using a quotation in the introduction.

We did this in class!

Directions: Write a three-sentence introduction for each topic below. At least one of the sentences should be a quotation. Remember that a quotation must have beginning and ending quotation marks and may have a "tag line," which tells who is speaking.

1. **If you could make one change at your school, what would it be?**

_____

_____

_____

_____

_____

2. **Tell a story about a time you had some bad luck.**

_____

_____

_____

_____

_____

Families, please help!

Directions: "We're off and running now!" Write a three-sentence introduction for each topic below. Make sure at least one of the sentences is a quotation. Remember that a quotation must have beginning and ending quotation marks and may have a "tag line," which tells who is speaking. Your responses do not have to be real; they can be fiction.

1. **Tell why a particular holiday is your favorite time of the year.**

_____

_____

_____

_____

_____

_____

2. **Tell what happened one time when you were lost.**

_____

_____

_____

_____

_____

_____

❋ **This assignment is due at school on** _____.

_____   _____
Child's name   Parent's signature

Week-by-Week Homework for Building Writing Skills © 2009 by Mary Rose, Scholastic Inc.

Dear Families,

Scribble, scribble, scribble! Erase, erase, erase! This is the sound of writing in our classroom. Children start to write, change their minds, erase, and write again. It is fascinating to watch them thinking on paper!

One easy way to begin an essay or story is to use sound or motion words, like in the above paragraph. Sound and motion words give readers a hint of where the story takes place, what action is occurring, or what the essay is about. They can be part of a whole sentence, but not necessarily. Notice that in addition to the motion words, the introduction above contains three sentences.

Today we practiced writing three-sentence introductions that include sound or motion words. Please take a few minutes to read the samples below so you can better help your child on tonight's homework.

Your Child's Teacher, _____

Writing Tip #5

To start an essay, try using sound or motion words to set the mood.

We did this in class!

Directions: Write a three-sentence introduction for each topic below. Your introduction should include words that indicate either sound or motion.

1. **What is your favorite game? Why is it your favorite?**

_____

_____

_____

_____

_____

2. **Tell a story about a time an animal did something funny.**

_____

_____

_____

_____

_____

Families, please help!

Directions: Toil! Grunt! Authors often choose to begin their writing with sound and motion words to set the mood. How did you feel when you read, "Toil! Grunt!"? Did you think you were in for hard work? Or did you think the writer was trying to be funny? Try to set a mood with your choice of sound or motion words. For each topic below, write a three-sentence introduction that includes sound or motion words.

1. **What animal would you choose for a pet? Why would you choose that animal?**

_____
_____
_____
_____
_____
_____

2. **Write a story about a time you rode something.**

_____
_____
_____
_____
_____
_____

❋ **This assignment is due at school on** _____ .

_____   _____
Child's name   Parent's signature

Dear Families,

Although there are many good ways to begin an essay or story, by far the most popular—and probably the easiest—is to "just start talking." This means simply beginning the piece without fanfare, without questions, quotes, or clever sound or motion words. This is demonstrated in the paragraph you are currently reading. Nothing fancy, just a simple explanation of a solid way to start writing.

Although this may seem like less work than other ways of beginning writing, students can be stymied by the utter simplicity of this technique. Help your child see that "start talking" is what he or she does every day … and that it is an easy and effective way to write an introduction.

Your Child's Teacher, _____

Writing Tip #6

To start an essay, sometimes you just need to start talking.

We did this in class!

Directions: Write an introduction for each of the topics listed below. Each paragraph should be at least three sentences long.

1. **Tell why computers are important to you.**

_____

_____

_____

_____

_____

2. **Write a story about a person in your family.**

_____

_____

_____

_____

_____

Families, please help!

Directions: Write a three-sentence introduction for each topic below. For each topic, show that you can begin an essay or story by simply starting to talk. In other words, just start writing. You do not always need to use clever techniques, such as quotations, questions, or sound words.

1. **What is the best book you have ever read? Write an essay to tell why you liked it.**

_____

_____

_____

_____

_____

_____

2. **Tell a story about a favorite day at school.**

_____

_____

_____

_____

_____

_____

❋ **This assignment is due at school on** _____ .

_____   _____
Child's name   Parent's signature

Week-by-Week Homework for Building Writing Skills © 2009 by Mary Rose, Scholastic Inc.

Dear Families,

I have chosen to give this assignment because we have a state writing assessment that requires students to write to a specific prompt. Sometimes students get stuck and have difficulty starting their writing. Since the assessment is a timed test, it is important that your child knows some strategies to get started right away.

One easy way to begin writing an essay or story is to restate the prompt. It may not be very exciting, but it is a solid, valid way to start writing, and your child will receive credit for writing an introduction. Restating the prompt means using the words in the prompt to create the introduction. These prompts are often written in three sentences, so the prompts you see here are in that format. Take a look at the samples we did in class today.

Your Child's Teacher, _____

Writing Tip

 # 7

What if you can't think of a good introduction? If all else fails, restate the prompt.

We did this in class!

Directions: Use the words in each prompt to write a three-sentence introduction for each topic.

1. **Most people have a favorite day of the week. What is your favorite day? Write an essay to explain why that day is your favorite.**

_____

_____

_____

_____

_____

2. **You are taking out the garbage. As you approach the garbage can, you suddenly see a bright green light in the sky. Write a story about what happens next.**

_____

_____

_____

_____

_____

_____

Families, please help!

Directions: Pretend that you are stuck and cannot think of a clever introduction for your state writing assessment. Use the words in each of these three-sentence prompts to create an introduction paragraph. You may not copy the sentences exactly as they are written.

1. **Most people have a favorite holiday or time of year. What is your favorite holiday? Write an essay to explain why a particular holiday or time of year is your favorite.**

_____

_____

_____

_____

_____

_____

2. **You are walking down the sidewalk when you suddenly find something interesting. What is it? What will happen if you pick it up? Write a story to tell what happened the day you found something interesting on the sidewalk.**

_____

_____

_____

_____

_____

_____

❋ **This assignment is due at school on** _____ .

_____   _____
Child's name   Parent's signature

        Week-by-Week Homework for Building Writing Skills © 2009 by Mary Rose, Scholastic Inc.

Dear Families,

Children often have difficulty deciding what to write for a topic sentence and how to follow that up with appropriate supporting details. Look at this example:

The truck was awesome. It was painted a bright blue with red and yellow flames down the sides. It had enormous tires, large enough for a man to stand in the center of them. The top of the cab had to be at least twenty-feet high. It sat out by the highway and everyone called it "Big Foot."

In this paragraph, "The truck was awesome" is the topic sentence. Everything else in the paragraph explains what about the truck made it so awesome. In elementary school, the topic sentence is usually the first sentence in the paragraph. See the samples we did in class today to help you understand the homework.

Your Child's Teacher, _____

Writing Tip #8

Write a clear topic sentence and support it with details.

We did this in class!

Directions: Write an appropriate topic sentence for the paragraph below.

_____

When I got to the finish line, I thought I would die. I crashed over the line and fell right on the ground. I was exhausted, but I won the 100-yard dash.

Directions: Write supporting details for this topic sentence.

You will not believe what is in my desk! _____

_____

_____

_____

_____

_____

_____

_____

_____

Families, please help!

Directions: Write an appropriate topic sentence for the paragraph below.

_____

We had fun setting up the tent and unfolding our sleeping bags. Then we went for a hike in the woods. We even saw a real live deer! When we got back to our camp we made a fire and roasted hot dogs. Then we sang some songs and told stories around the campfire. It was a great night.

Directions: Write supporting details to go with this topic sentence.

It was the best meal I ever ate! _____

_____

_____

_____

_____

_____

_____

_____

_____

❋ **This assignment is due at school on** _____ .

_____   _____
Child's name   Parent's signature

Week-by-Week Homework for Building Writing Skills © 2009 by Mary Rose, Scholastic Inc.

Dear Families,

The topic sentence is often the first sentence in a paragraph. It indicates what the rest of the paragraph will be about. For example, I might start off with this topic sentence: *I love your outfit.* If I then continue to tell you what I like about it, these would be supporting details: *Those blue shoes go well with that purse. I love the length of your skirt, and that scarf really sets the whole thing off. Those earrings are a good choice, too.* All of these supporting details explain why I love your outfit.

But most paragraphs need a closing sentence, too. For beginning writers, this is probably the most difficult part of the whole essay. An easy way to help students learn to do this is to have them restate the topic sentence again using different words. A good closing sentence for the example above might be: *You look really great in those clothes.*

Your Child's Teacher, _____

Writing Tip

#9

Write a closing sentence for your paragraph.

We did this in class!

Directions: Write a topic sentence and a closing sentence for the following paragraph:

_____

While Mr. Catogni got out the clay, everyone put on smocks and got quiet. Then he showed us how to roll the clay like a snake and curl it around into a pot. He let us roll out clay and make our own pots. Mr. Catogni says we can fire our pots in the kiln.

_____

Directions: Write supporting details for this topic sentence and closing sentence. HINT: It can be fiction!

Last week we had the easiest assignment ever. _____

_____

_____

_____

_____

_____

_____ **I wish we had more easy assignments like this one!**

Families, please help!

Directions: Write a topic sentence and closing sentence for the following paragraph.

_____

First, I forgot to set my alarm, so I got up late. Then, my brother was yelling at me to hurry up. I tripped over the dog and skinned my knee as I was running to get in the car. When I finally got to school, I realized that I had forgotten my homework.

_____

Directions: Write supporting details for this topic sentence and closing sentence.

Boy, did that ever hurt! _____

_____

_____

_____

_____

_____

_____

_____

_____ **I will remember this pain for a long time.**

❄ **This assignment is due at school on** _____ .

_____   _____
Child's name   Parent's signature

          Week-by-Week Homework for Building Writing Skills © 2009 by Mary Rose, Scholastic Inc.

Dear Families,

When teachers or scorers of state writing assessments look at your child's writing, one of the elements they hope to find is evidence that the essay is whole and complete. That means the story or essay should not leave the reader wondering how the story ends or if there is another page still to come. When the reader reads the closing, he or she should instinctively know that it is the end.

There are many ways to accomplish this goal, but perhaps the easiest way for students is called "writing in a circle." This means that an effective closing simply takes a word, an idea, or a name from the introduction and reuses it in the conclusion. Be sure to read the examples below before you begin tonight's homework.

Write in a circle to make your piece feel whole and complete.

Your Child's Teacher, _____

We did this in class!

Directions: For each essay, read the introduction and write a three-sentence closing. Be sure to use at least one thing from the introduction in your conclusion.

1. **Introduction:** "Buddies and pals!" That is what Donna and I always say whenever we meet. We have been friends since we were three. Donna is a good friend to me, and this essay will tell why I think she is special.

    Closing: _____
    _____
    _____
    _____
    _____

2. **Introduction:** Have you ever lost a tooth? Did it bleed everywhere? Wait until you read what happened to me one day in kindergarten. It was a bloody day I will never forget.

    Closing: _____
    _____
    _____
    _____
    _____

Families, please help!

Directions: Today's writing lesson is about writing good conclusions by "writing in a circle." Read the introductions below. Then use at least one word, idea, or name from the introduction to write a three-sentence conclusion to these essays.

1. **Introduction:** "Go, Panthers!" That's what all of us say at Poston Elementary School. It is the best school in our whole county—maybe in the whole state! Read this essay to find out what makes our school so special.

Closing: _____

_____

_____

_____

_____

_____

_____

2. **Introduction:** There were 24 kids packed and ready to go on a one-hour bus ride to the science center. This was going to be an exciting day for us third graders. But there was more to the science center than I had ever imagined. Wait until you read what happened to us!

Closing: _____

_____

_____

_____

_____

_____

_____

❋ **This assignment is due at school on** _____ .

_____   _____
Child's name   Parent's signature

Week-by-Week Homework for Building Writing Skills © 2009 by Mary Rose, Scholastic Inc.

Section 2
Improving Your Writing

Dear Teachers,

I hope your students have found success with the first lessons and are ready to move on to the next writing steps. While I strongly suggest that you complete Section 1 first, Sections 2, 3, and 4 can easily be taught in any order to suit the needs of your students.

The first part of this book focused on the basic five-paragraph format. I would like to emphasize that this "formula writing" is merely a starting point. This format is especially effective for students who need to pass a state assessment or who are struggling with the basics of writing. Once they've become more experienced writers, they can deviate from this five-paragraph formula and create all kinds of wonderful essays and stories.

In this second part of the book, students will work on key skills, such as expanding simple sentences and using more precise words (instead of *stuff, things,* and *some*). This section contains eight lessons. Please continue to write full essays while you are assigning these for the next eight weeks. Remember, these homework activities are meant to supplement your writing program, not replace it. Enjoy!

Mary

Writing Tip #11

Use different types of sentences when you write.

Test scorers, teachers, and other professionals who assess writing advise students to use a variety of sentences in their writing. But students often do not know what this means.

In this lesson, we look at four types of sentences—statement, question, exclamation, and command. Invite students to give examples of each type of sentence and write them on the board. Remind them that sentences always start with a capital letter and end with appropriate punctuation. A statement ends with a period, a question with a question mark, and an exclamation with an exclamation point. Commands are a little trickier. A "soft command," like a request (Pass the salt.), can end with a period, while a demand (Throw the ball to first base!) ends with an exclamation point.

Hand out copies of the homework sheet (page 45) and have students practice writing each of the four types of sentences.

Note: Caution students not to force every type of sentence into a paragraph or their writing will sound stilted and contrived.

"We did this in class" sample answers:

1. **Statement:** Mrs. Doerr is absent today, so our class will have a substitute teacher.

   Question: Do you know who the substitute will be?

   Exclamation: I hope our substitute is not Miss Viola Swamp!

   Command: Tell me if you know who it is.

2. **Statement:** Today is a special day for me.

   Question: Did you know that it is my birthday?

   Exclamation: I am finally ten!

   Command: Bring on the cake!

Writing Tip #**12**

Vary the lengths of your sentences.

Explain to students that simply varying the length of their sentences can make their writing more interesting to read. Write the following paragraph on the board:

What a storm! It rained endlessly last night. Thunder boomed and lightning crashed all evening long and into the dead of the night.

Ask students to look for a short sentence, a long sentence, and a sentence fragment in the paragraph. Explain that a sentence fragment is a group of words that lacks either a subject or a verb.

Hand out copies of the homework sheet (page 47) and have students practice writing sentences of different lengths. Warn them, however, that when they write a sentence fragment, they should make sure that it is on topic and goes with their other two sentences. In other words, it should make sense.

"We did this in class" sample answers:

Angel food cake is my favorite dessert. I like it because it is so light and fluffy it seems to be floating on a cloud and is low in calories. Tastes good too!

Blood everywhere! I was trying to slice a tomato to put on my toasted bacon, lettuce, and tomato sandwich when the knife slipped and sliced right into the index finger of my left hand. This is going to need stitches!

Writing Tip #13

Liven up your writing by using exciting verbs.

When we hear the word *verb*, we naturally think of action words. Unfortunately, students tend to use the same verbs over and over again, making for boring conversation and writing. Beyond the boredom factor, the least sophisticated words hardly do justice to exciting action.

On the board, write this sentence: *The crowd <u>moved</u> toward the theater.* Invite students to replace the word *moved* with more exciting verbs (for example, *clambered, shuffled, shoved, snaked,* or *pushed*). Explain that when writers substitute exciting verbs for boring ones, the overall quality of the writing improves. Hand out copies of the homework sheet (page 49).

"We did this in class" sample answers:

run	eat	write	make
1. dash	1. gobble	1. scribble	1. create
2. scoot	2. swallow	2. jot	2. design
3. hurry	3. chew	3. inscribe	3. construct
4. sprint	4. munch	4. print	4. build

1. Michael crashed his bicycle into a tree.

2. The pirate dived from his ship and splashed into the water.

3. When the teacher noticed that the girls were chewing gum, she marched across the room to scold them.

Writing Tip #14

Spice up your writing by using descriptive adjectives.

An adjective is any word that describes a noun (a person, place, or thing). Students overuse boring adjectives the same way they overuse boring verbs.

Choose a wall or bulletin board in your classroom and post some boring adjectives, such as *good, fun,* and *nice* across the top. Then ask students to brainstorm more descriptive adjectives that they might use in place of these words. Explain that words that mean the same or almost the same thing are called synonyms. Encourage students to add synonyms to the list throughout the school year. Students will constantly be on the lookout for great words that they can add to the wall. This might even inspire a memorable thesaurus or dictionary lesson! Hand out copies of the homework sheet (page 51).

Tip

Just before students hand in their completed writing assignments, have them reread their piece and look for three boring verbs. Have them erase these words and replace them with more exciting, more vivid verbs.

Tip

Just before students hand in their completed writing assignments, have them reread the piece and look for three boring adjectives. Have them erase these words and replace them with more exciting, more descriptive adjectives.

"We did this in class" sample answers:

big	cold	hard	pretty
1. enormous	1. chilly	1. difficult	1. beautiful
2. huge	2. freezing	2. tricky	2. gorgeous
3. large	3. icy	3. demanding	3. lovely
4. gigantic	4. frosty	4. challenging	4. attractive

1. Our principal was astounded by our excellent scores on the state tests.

2. Fido barked nervously when he heard a piercing noise outside the door.

3. Tommy stared at the towering, terrifying monster with hideous teeth.

Writing Tip #15

Try to be specific when you are writing. Avoid using general words like *stuff*, *things*, and *some*.

Teaching students to be specific can be quite a challenge. Sometimes a non-example is the best way to teach a concept. Have a conversation with students in which you use very general words and terms. For example:

"Boys and girls, today we are going to do some stuff in math. We will use some materials to help you learn new and difficult things. When we finish there will be a test in which you will be expected to explain everything and use the correct terms and spell them correctly. Any questions?"

Continue along these lines for a few more minutes to help students see that in order to make ourselves clearly understood, we need to use specific words. Students who engage in peer editing can ask each other questions about what they have read. If the reader has many questions about the essay, then that is a signal to the author that he or she has not been specific enough.

Hand out copies of the homework sheet (page 53). Consider doing a whole-group activity to rewrite the story. Encourage students to add new sentences to make the story more interesting.

"We did this in class" sample answer:

Last July, a boy **named Timothy** was feeling very unhappy because **he had just moved to a new town. He missed his best friend Jason, and he missed being on the Tigers baseball team.** One morning, he walked into **the kitchen** to find a **brand-new golden retriever puppy** waiting for him. The **puppy** made him feel **excited. He forgot about feeling lonely.** He was no longer sad. Now he felt **thrilled** because **the puppy licked his face and wagged his tail and made him feel loved.** At last **Timothy** felt happy again.

Writing Tip #16

Expand simple sentences by using adjectives, adverbs, and prepositional phrases.

Beginning writers naturally write in short, simple sentences, such as: *I have a new dog. His name is Benjy. He sleeps on my bed.* As students gain more competence in writing, encourage them to expand their sentences so that they flow and sound more interesting.

Start by writing a simple sentence on the board, such as: *The lion roared.* Invite students to expand the sentence by adding an adjective. Remind them that an adjective is a word that describes a noun. Ask, "What adjective can we use to describe the lion?" Under the simple sentence, write a second sentence with the added word. For example: *The **enormous** lion roared.*

Next, ask students to add an adverb to describe the verb *roared.* Explain that adverbs often end in *-ly.* Write the new, longer sentence under the second sentence: *The enormous lion roared **loudly.***

Finally, have students think of a prepositional phrase to go with the sentence. Explain that a prepositional phrase begins with a preposition, such as *on, under,* or *by,* and often tells where or when an action happens. Your fourth sentence could read: *The enormous lion roared loudly **inside the cave.*** Notice that the four sentences look like a pyramid:

The lion roared.

*The **enormous** lion roared.*

*The enormous lion roared **loudly**.*

*The enormous lion roared loudly **inside the cave**.*

Hand out copies of the homework sheet (page 55). You may want to complete the in-class activity as a whole-group lesson. Then invite the class to work in small groups to create more pyramids. Allow students to illustrate their sentences, read them out loud, and display them on a bulletin board.

"We did this in class" sample answers:

The **skinny** boy walked **quickly across the icy pond to get to the mall**.
The **tiny** girl laughed **loudly in the car as they drove to the circus**.

Writing Tip #17

When writing an expository or narrative essay, avoid using the word *you.*

Students in my fourth-grade class often have difficulty staying in a consistent "person" when writing. They might begin a piece in the first person (*I, we, us*) and then suddenly change to the second person, *you*. I have tried to tell them that I was not in the dungeon or riding the roller coaster, but they don't seem to get it. So I tell them to write the whole essay without using the word *you*.

Hand out copies of the homework sheet (page 57). Read the story aloud then ask students to replace the words *you* and *your* with more appropriate words.

"We did this in class" sample answers:

The school had a "dungeon" under the stair steps. If **children** were bad, the teachers made **them** go under the stairs and stay there all day. If **they** got sent to the dungeon three times, **they** got expelled from school. Then **they** would have to tell **their** parents that **they** were not allowed to come back to school. It would be terrible for **boys and girls** to be in the dungeon.

Writing Tip #18

Set the tone of your writing by using alternatives to the word *said*.

Write this sentence on the board: *"There is no school tomorrow,"* <u>*said*</u> *Nancy*. Ask students: What other words can we use to replace the word *said*? Make a list of all the words students volunteer. Add some yourself, if necessary.

Guide students to notice that some words can add emotion to a sentence. To demonstrate, use colored markers to categorize the words according to mood. For example, what alternative words could show that Nancy felt sad that there was no school? (*Moaned, wailed, cried*) What if she felt angry? (*Yelled, screamed, hissed*) Happy? (*Giggled, shrieked, exclaimed*) Hand out copies of the homework sheet (page 59) and complete the activity as a class.

"We did this in class" sample answers:

Scene #1:

"Michael just hit a home run," cheered Tiara.

"I didn't see him do it," wailed Carlie.

"The Tigers are ahead by one run," exclaimed Jordan.

"They can win the championship game," cried Ben.

"Michael is a hero," squealed Mikayla.

Scene #2:

"Michael just hit a home run," groaned Cathy.

"I didn't see him do it," objected Joann.

"The Tigers are ahead by one run," grumbled Jamie.

"They can win the championship game," gasped Brando.

"Michael is a hero," sneered Allison.

Dear Families,

You should practice writing every day. So get busy. Your writing can be super! What are you waiting for?

Did you notice that the above paragraph used four different types of sentences? The first sentence was a statement, the second was a command, the third was an exclamation, and the fourth was a question. Using various types of sentences makes our writing more interesting and enjoyable to read. This is not to say that students should use all four types of sentences in every piece—the writing might then feel contrived and unnatural.

Today's homework asks students to practice writing all four types of sentences. Take a look at the activity below to help you understand the homework.

Your Child's Teacher, _____

Use different types of sentences when you write.

We did this in class!

Directions: Read the topics below and then write four different types of sentences that might tell about this topic. Here is an example to get you started:

Topic: You are going swimming.

Statement: I am putting on my new swimsuit.

Question: Do you have a new suit, too?

Exclamation: What a great color!

Command: Jump in, the water's great!

Topic: You have a substitute teacher today.

Statement: _____

Question: _____

Exclamation: _____

Command: _____

Topic: It is your birthday.

Statement: _____

Question: _____

Exclamation: _____

Command: _____

Families, please help!

Directions: Read each of the topics below. Then write a statement, a question, an exclamation, and a command for each one. Be sure to use a capital letter at the beginning of each sentence and the correct ending punctuation (period, question mark, or exclamation point).

Topic: There will be no school tomorrow because of bad weather.

Statement: ____________________

Question: ____________________

Exclamation: ____________________

Command: ____________________

Topic: Your team just won the county championship.

Statement: ____________________

Question: ____________________

Exclamation: ____________________

Command: ____________________

Topic: Your dog just ate your hamburger.

Statement: ____________________

Question: ____________________

Exclamation: ____________________

Command: ____________________

This assignment is due at school on ____________________.

Child's name ____________________

Parent's signature ____________________

Week-by-Week Homework for Building Writing Skills © 2009 by Mary Rose, Scholastic Inc.

Dear Families,

Authors try very hard to keep their readers interested in what they have written so that they will continue reading and enjoying the short story, essay, or article all the way to the very last word. They do this in many ways. They might use humor. Or interesting language. Another technique is using variety in the length of their sentences—as was done in this paragraph.

In today's homework, your child will write three sentences on a familiar topic. One sentence should be quite long, the other very short, and the third should be a sentence fragment. A sentence fragment is a group of words that lacks a subject, a verb, or both. Remind your child that the fragment must be on topic and fit with the other two sentences.

Your Child's Teacher, _____

Vary the lengths of your sentences.

 We did this in class!

Directions: Write one long sentence, one short sentence, and a sentence fragment for each topic below. Remember, a sentence fragment is a group of words that lacks a subject, a verb, or both. Try to make the fragment work with the other two sentences so the paragraph makes sense.

Topic: **Describe a delicious dessert.**

_____

_____

_____

_____

_____

Topic: **You just cut your finger.**

_____

_____

_____

_____

_____

Families, please help!

Directions: Write one long sentence, one short sentence, and a sentence fragment for each topic below. Remember, a sentence fragment is a group of words that lacks a subject, a verb, or both. Try to make the fragment work with the other two sentences so the paragraph makes sense.

Topic: **You are enjoying a cool drink on a hot day.**

_____

_____

_____

_____

_____

Topic: **Someone just stole your bicycle.**

_____

_____

_____

_____

_____

Topic: **Describe your bedroom.**

_____

_____

_____

_____

_____

❋ **This assignment is due at school on** _____ .

_____   _____
Child's name   Parent's signature

          Week-by-Week Homework for Building Writing Skills © 2009 by Mary Rose, Scholastic Inc.

Dear Families,

Many of the verbs in our language show action. We can tell about that action either by using boring words or by employing vivid verbs. Today's homework is in two parts: First, students list alternatives for boring verbs. Then, students rewrite sentences and replace boring verbs with more exciting ones. Whenever you are helping your child with writing assignments, try to encourage him or her to add interest to their work by using lively verbs.

Your Child's Teacher, _____

Liven up your writing by using exciting verbs.

We did this in class!

Directions: Exciting verbs show action. Under each boring verb write four livelier verbs that have the same meaning.

run	eat	write	make
1. _____	1. _____	1. _____	1. _____
2. _____	2. _____	2. _____	2. _____
3. _____	3. _____	3. _____	3. _____
4. _____	4. _____	4. _____	4. _____

Directions: Replace the **boldfaced** boring verbs with livelier, more precise ones.

1. Michael **rode** his bicycle into a tree.

_____

2. The pirate **got off** his ship and **went** into the water.

_____

3. When the teacher **saw** that the girls were chewing gum, she **went** across the room to **talk to** them.

_____

_____

Families, please help!

Directions: Under each boring verb write four more exciting verbs that could be used in their place. Feel free to use a dictionary or thesaurus for this activity.

move	speak	hit	look
1. _____	1. _____	1. _____	1. _____
2. _____	2. _____	2. _____	2. _____
3. _____	3. _____	3. _____	3. _____
4. _____	4. _____	4. _____	4. _____

Directions: Replace the **boldfaced** boring verbs with livelier, more precise ones.

1. The entire football team **went** onto the field when they won the championship.

   _____

2. Emily **cut** open the contest envelope to see if she had won a prize.

   _____

3. All of a sudden the computer **moved** across the desk.

   _____

4. The cat **walked** across the top of the couch, **looking** down at the dog below.

   _____

Bonus: Write one fabulous original sentence with an exciting verb in it.

   _____

❋ **This assignment is due at school on** _____ .

_____   _____
Child's name   Parent's signature

Week-by-Week Homework for Building Writing Skills © 2009 by Mary Rose, Scholastic Inc.

Dear Families,

Your child has moved beyond the primary grades so it is time for him or her to begin using adjectives that are more descriptive than *good, fun,* and *nice*. This writing activity is designed to help your child think of better alternatives to these overused words. You are welcome to use a thesaurus or dictionary if you and your child are having trouble coming up with words. Please use the word *synonym* to describe words that mean the same or almost the same thing. For example, *big* is a synonym for *large*.

Your Child's Teacher, _____

Spice up your writing by using descriptive adjectives.

We did this in class!

Directions: Under each boring adjective, list four words that are more exciting and have the same or nearly the same meaning.

big	cold	hard	pretty
1. _____	1. _____	1. _____	1. _____
2. _____	2. _____	2. _____	2. _____
3. _____	3. _____	3. _____	3. _____
4. _____	4. _____	4. _____	4. _____

Directions: Replace the **boldfaced** words with more exciting, more descriptive adjectives. You can alter the sentence if you wish.

1. Our principal was astounded by our **good** scores on the state tests.

   _____

2. Fido barked nervously when he heard a **loud** noise outside the door.

   _____

3. Tommy stared at the **big, scary** monster with **ugly** teeth.

   _____

Families, please help!

Directions: Under each boring adjective, list four words that are more exciting and have the same or nearly the same meaning. Feel free to use a dictionary or thesaurus to help you.

loud	ugly	scary	happy
1. _____	1. _____	1. _____	1. _____
2. _____	2. _____	2. _____	2. _____
3. _____	3. _____	3. _____	3. _____
4. _____	4. _____	4. _____	4. _____

Directions: Replace the **boldfaced** words with more exciting, more descriptive adjectives. You can alter the sentence if you wish.

1. All of us think that Mrs. Blake is a **nice** teacher.

   _____

2. When you play the trumpet, it sounds very **loud**.

   _____

3. I want to win a prize for the **ugliest** costume.

   _____

4. I was **happy** when my dad won the lottery.

   _____

5. Singing in public is **scary**.

   _____

❋ **This assignment is due at school on** _____ .

_____   _____
Child's name   Parent's signature

   Week-by-Week Homework for Building Writing Skills © 2009 by Mary Rose, Scholastic Inc.

Dear Families,

Some children have trouble using good words in their writing. They tend to overuse words like *stuff* and *things*. They need to improve their writing. They need better words to make their writing better.

Did you notice that the above paragraph seemed unclear? Vague words, such as *some*, *good*, and *better*, are not specific and can leave a reader baffled.

Many students use vague words in their writing because that is how they talk. They may also not know how to spell more difficult words or lack the vocabulary to use more sophisticated words. Whatever the reason, all writers need to work on being specific. Please help your child replace vague words with more specific words that will make the story clearer for the reader.

Your Child's Teacher, _____

Try to be specific when you are writing. Avoid using general words like *stuff*, *things*, and *some*.

We did this in class!

Directions: Rewrite the story below, replacing the **boldfaced** words with more specific ones. Feel free to add other sentences to make your story more detailed. Have fun with this assignment.

One time *(when?)*, **a boy** *(who?)* was feeling very unhappy because a lot of **bad stuff** *(what bad stuff?)* had happened to him. One morning, he walked into **a room** *(what room?)* to find **a new pet** *(what pet?)* waiting for him. The **pet** made him feel **different** *(what emotions?)*. He was no longer sad. Now he felt **better** *(how did he feel?)* because the **pet had done something** *(what?)* to **change his mood**. At last the **boy** felt happy again.

_____

_____

_____

_____

_____

_____

_____

_____

_____

_____

Families, please help!

Directions: Rewrite the story below, replacing the **boldfaced** words with more specific ones. You can make the story happen any place you want and make it funny, sad, scary, or happy. You can also exaggerate so that the story is not realistic at all! Try not to repeat the same words in the story. Feel free to add other sentences to make your story more detailed. Have fun with this assignment.

The girl *(who?)* looked **out**. *(Out what? A window? What else can you look out of?)* She could tell she was not on Earth. She saw **stuff** *(what stuff?)* floating by **doing funny things**. *(What was it doing?)* She could smell something **strange**. *(How did it smell?)* She could hear a **noise**. *(What noise?)* The noise made her think about **something**. *(What?)* Then she felt **movement**. *(What kind of movement? How could she be moving?)* Suddenly she realized she was not alone. **Someone** *(who?)* was there with her, and the **person** *(who?)* was **talking**. *(What was he or she saying?)*

_____

_____

_____

_____

_____

_____

_____

_____

_____

_____

_____

_____

_____

❋ **This assignment is due at school on** _____ .

_____   _____
Child's name   Parent's signature

   Week-by-Week Homework for Building Writing Skills © 2009 by Mary Rose, Scholastic Inc.

Dear Families,

Sometimes it is acceptable, even desirable, for authors to write very short sentences. We like them. Short sentences break up the flow of writing and give the reader a chance to pause—just like you did when you read, "We like them." But it is not desirable for a child to write *only* short sentences.

This homework assignment is designed to help your child expand his or her sentences in an easy way. We begin with a few short sentences and then expand them by adding an adjective (a word that describes a noun), an adverb (a word that describes a verb), and a prepositional phrase (a phrase that begins with a preposition, such as *on*, *under*, and *by*, and tells where or when the action happened). Check out what we did in class today.

Your Child's Teacher, _____

Writing Tip #16

Expand simple sentences by using adjectives, adverbs, and prepositional phrases.

We did this in class!

Directions: Read these short sentences. Then build a pyramid to make the sentences longer by adding adjectives, adverbs, and prepositional phrases.

The boy walked.

The _____ boy walked.
(adjective)

The _____ boy walked _____.
(adverb)

The _____ boy walked _____ _____.
(prepositional phrase)

The _____ boy walked _____ _____ _____.
(Even longer!)

The girl laughed.

The _____ girl laughed.
(adjective)

The _____ girl laughed _____.
(adverb)

The _____ girl laughed _____ _____.
(prepositional phrase)

The _____ girl laughed _____ _____ _____.
(Even longer!)

Writing Tip **#16**

Directions: Read the short sentences below. Expand each sentence by adding an adjective, an adverb, and a prepositional phrase. Notice how your writing becomes more interesting as you add these details. Have fun with this assignment.

A kite flew.

A _____ kite flew.
          (adjective)

A _____ kite flew _____.
                                                    (adverb)

A _____ kite flew _____ _____.
                                                    (prepositional phrase)

The snake slithered.

The _____ snake slithered.
            (adjective)

The _____ snake slithered _____.
                                                        (adverb)

The _____ snake slithered _____ _____.
                                                        (prepositional phrase)

Directions: Now that you have practiced, expand each short sentence below into a long sentence. Can you make them even longer than the examples above?

The bubble popped.

_____

The pennies spilled.

_____

❋ **This assignment is due at school on** _____.

_____   _____
          Child's name   Parent's signature

Week-by-Week Homework for Building Writing Skills © 2009 by Mary Rose, Scholastic Inc.

Dear Families,

Students in elementary schools learn how to write both expository and narrative essays. Expository essays are written to inform, while narratives tell a story. Most children can write both types of essays, but they often switch "person" while they are writing.

In today's sample essay Daniel begins his paragraph in the first person, using *our, we, my,* and *I.* Halfway through the paragraph, however, he starts explaining about how children were punished long ago. Instead of using the third person (*they, them,* or *the children*), he switched to the second person and used *you.* When he did this, the paragraph stopped making sense because obviously it is not the reader who is in the dungeon. See how we fixed the essay below so you can help your child with the homework on the next page.

Your Child's Teacher, _____

When writing an expository or narrative essay, avoid using the word *you.*

We did this in class!

Daniel writes:

Our class went on a great history field trip. We went to St. Augustine, Florida, the oldest city in America. While we were in St. Augustine, we visited the Oldest Wooden Schoolhouse in America. My favorite part was the wax figures that could talk. I also saw how they punished kids back then.

** The school had a "dungeon" under the stair steps. If you were bad, the teachers made you go under the stairs and stay there all day. If you got sent to the dungeon three times, you got expelled from school. Then you would have to tell your parents that you were not allowed to come back to school. It would be terrible for you to be in the dungeon.

Directions: Start from the ** and rewrite the paragraph by changing the word *you* to *them, they, the children,* or *the boys and girls.* The story should now make more sense since *you* were never in the dungeon—we hope!

_____

_____

_____

_____

_____

_____

_____

_____

Families, please help!

Directions: Read the passage below. Starting from the **, rewrite the second paragraph without using the word *you*. Use first-person pronouns such as *I, we, our,* and *us.*

My family loves roller coasters. We love to ride them at the county fair, at Disney World, and at amusement parks, such as Coney Island and Six Flags. We all pile into the roller coasters—even my mom—and then scream the whole time we are on.

The best roller coaster I have ever been on is ShieKra at Busch Gardens in Tampa. ** First, they put you in the seat and strap the seatbelt tightly around you. As you start to move, you soon realize that you are in for a wild ride. When you get to the very top, you tip over the edge but you don't come crashing down like on other roller coasters. Instead, you go over the edge and then the whole car jerks around while you are staring straight down at the ground. You feel like you are going to die as everyone starts screaming around you. Finally, you rush down toward the end. That is when you know that ShieKra is the best roller coaster of all!

_____

_____

_____

_____

_____

_____

_____

_____

_____

_____

_____

_____

_____

This assignment is due at school on _____ .

_____   _____
Child's name   Parent's signature

Dear Families,

There are many alternatives to the word *said*. Writers can set the tone of their writing by choosing other words that convey emotion, such as anger, humor, suspense, or fear. Consider the following sentence: *"Let the dog out, Carol," said David.* The word *said* implies that David is simply speaking without much emotion. What happens when we replace the word *said*?

"Let the dog out, Carol!" demanded David.

"Let the dog out, Carol," begged David.

"Let the dog out, Carol," whispered David.

Now we have three different tones to our writing. When David is demanding, we feel a sense of urgency. When he is begging, we may begin to wonder why. When he is whispering, we feel a sense of suspense and quiet.

When your child is writing, please help him or her find alternatives to the word *said*. It will enrich the essay and add to the overall quality of the story.

Your Child's Teacher, _____

Writing Tip #18

Set the tone of your writing by using alternatives to the word *said*.

We did this in class!

Directions: Fill in the blanks with words that mean the same or nearly the same as *said*. Make sure the words you choose convey an appropriate mood for the conversation. (HINT: Read the whole passage before you begin to work.)

Scene #1: These children are cheering for the Tigers to win the baseball game.

"Michael just hit a home run," _____ Tiara.

"I didn't see him do it," _____ Carlie.

"The Tigers are ahead by one run," _____ Jordan.

"They can win the championship game," _____ Ben.

"Michael is a hero," _____ Mikayla.

Scene #2: These children do not want the Tigers to win the baseball game.

"Michael just hit a home run," _____ Cathy.

"I didn't see him do it," _____ Joann.

"The Tigers are ahead by one run," _____ Jamie.

"They can win the championship game," _____ Brando.

"Michael is a hero," _____ Allison.

Families, please help!

Directions: Fill in the blanks with words that mean the same or nearly the same as *said*. Make sure the words you choose convey an appropriate mood for the conversation. (HINT: Read the whole passage before you begin to work.)

"I just spilled the paint," _____ Mark.

"Let's clean it up quickly," _____ Corey.

"I'm going to tell on you," _____ Jamie.

"Here comes the teacher," _____ Julie.

"I think we have a problem," _____ Heidi.

"I'm tired," _____ Benny.

"Let's go straight to bed," _____ his brother Jake.

"Did you just hear a noise?" _____ Benny.

"Yes, I think it was a door," _____ Jake.

"It's creaking like someone is opening it," _____ Benny.

"Do you hear footsteps?" _____ Benny.

"Something is coming upstairs," _____ Jake.

"Something is coming in our room," _____ Benny.

"I feel something on my bed," _____ Jake.

"Turn on the light," _____ Benny.

"It's only the dog," _____ Jake.

"I never knew he could open doors," _____ Benny.

On a separate sheet of paper, write your own conversation—at least five sentences—about a topic of your choice. Do not use the word *said*. Try to let the reader know the mood of your story. Are your characters happy, sad, frightened, suspicious, angry, or do they have another mood?

❋ **This assignment is due at school on** _____ .

_____   _____

Child's name   Parent's signature

Week-by-Week Homework for Building Writing Skills © 2009 by Mary Rose, Scholastic Inc.

Section 3
Adding Zing to Your Writing

Dear Teachers,

It is not enough for students to simply write a five-paragraph essay. This format is merely a starting point for beginning writers. In this section, students will learn how to add elaborations, content, and supporting details to expand their pieces to six-, seven-, or eight-paragraph essays. Longer, more complicated essays give students a chance to showcase their skills and often mean higher scores on state writing assessments.

Writing Tips #19 to #22 are designed for narrative writing. In each mini-lesson, students will "push the pause button" on the video that is playing in their heads as they write their stories. Then they will describe what they see. Most students tend to describe only physical characteristics, but this section will help them also describe scenes, actions, and characters' thoughts.

Writing Tips #23 and #24 focus on expository writing. In an expository essay, elaboration paragraphs can use description, as in narrative essays, or can give a specific example or tell a mini-story or vignette.

For all of these elaboration paragraphs, I provide paragraph starters, also known as *transition words*. Students will do well to remember them and use them often.

Good luck with teaching your students to add these elaboration, content, and supporting-detail paragraphs to their writing!

Mary

Writing Tip #19

In a narrative essay, elaborate by writing a whole paragraph that describes the physical characteristics of someone or something in the story.

When we ask students to describe something, the least-experienced writers begin with the five senses. They tell us what things look like, feel like, smell like, taste like, and sound like. This is an excellent place to begin, but as students develop more writing skills, they need to learn about more sophisticated ways to describe.

Moving students to the second level of description means getting them to include more specific words. Instead of saying something "smelled good," they could say, "It smelled of cinnamon." Rather than simply stating that something is a big box, students could specify its size, color, and shape: "It was a huge, brown, rectangular box the size of a refrigerator."

The third level of description is when students use similes and metaphors: "It smelled like Grandma's apple pie kitchen." "The brown refrigerator box was a huge cavern to the small boy."

Modeling and providing examples will go a long way in helping students move up this ladder of description skills.

When you start this lesson, have students choose a character from their earliest reading days—Cinderella, Nate the Great, or Winn-Dixie the dog. It's best if the character comes from picture books or has been featured on screen, so the class can generally agree on how to describe the character. More advanced students can write about characters they have not yet seen.

Hand out copies of the homework sheet (page 67). Teach students to describe people from top to bottom and animals from nose to tail. This way, they can "run their eyes" down the imaginary or real person and describe everything they see. One problem I have with my own class is that students often confuse "describing" with "listing." You may have to help your students see the difference between these two skills.

"We did this in class" sample answers:

I choose to describe Miss Viola Swamp from *Miss Nelson Is Missing*. Miss Swamp's hair is long and straight and black. It almost covers her face, which has a huge nose right in the middle of it. She is always frowning and wears black lipstick to match her long black fingernails. All of Miss Swamp's clothes are black and long and dreary looking. She is creepy right down to her black high-heeled shoes.

Writing Tip #20

In a narrative essay, elaborate by writing a whole paragraph that describes a scene or a room.

This lesson is similar to Writing Tip #19, except that students will describe either a scene or a room. When students describe a scene or a room, do not allow them just to make a list of what is there. They need to write a genuine description; encourage them to provide numbers, colors, sizes, and shapes, and to include sights, smells, sounds, and even tastes.

To begin the lesson, take students to the front of your school or to the playground and have them look around carefully. Then have them describe in detail what they see as they move their eyes around, starting from one spot. This will help them get ready for the on-paper task of describing their own classroom. Hand out copies of the homework sheet (page 69).

"We did this in class" sample answer:

When we enter the classroom, we immediately notice the shelves to the left. They are jammed full of lunch boxes, backpacks, violins, and sports equipment. As we look around the room, we see floor-to-ceiling bookshelves and a counter with class pet cages spread out all over it. Next to the teacher's messy desk, we see chalkboards and storage cupboards overflowing with papers, toys, and science projects. Finally, we see the only neat place in the classroom—the computer stations. Each white, shiny Macintosh computer is clean, dust-free, and blinking for students' attention.

Writing Tip #21

In a narrative essay, elaborate by writing a whole paragraph that describes the action.

Most students, especially boys, like to describe action. One problem they often have, however, is that they are merely listing a series of events rather than actually describing the action. For example:

The evil Martian hit Stephen. Then Stephen kicked him. The Martian hit him again. Stephen took out his laser gun. The Martian shot the laser out of Stephen's hand. Stephen ran into the vault and shut the door.

One easy way to make sure actions are more fully described is to have students include some adverbs. Adverbs modify verbs and, in this case, help tell how the action happened. Including prepositional phrases will also give the paragraph more meaning. Add more adjectives, sentence variation, and more specific words, and we get a decent descriptive paragraph.

*The evil Martian **suddenly** hit Stephen **in the head**. Then Stephen kicked him **soundly on the shoulder**. **But** the Martian hit him **in the head again**. **Stephen screamed in pain. At last,** Stephen took out his **Pulsar** laser gun. The Martian shot the laser out of Stephen's hand, **and it tumbled out of reach**. Stephen **ducked** into the vault and **slammed** the door.*

Hand out copies of the homework sheet (page 71). One fun way to teach how to describe action is to stage an event in your classroom, perhaps with the help of a colleague. Have your accomplice come in and do something unusual, like erase the chalkboard, write an unusual message, and then leave. Work with the whole class to create a paragraph that describes what they just witnessed. Encourage students to describe how the person walked, how he acted, what he said and did, and what finally happened. (CAUTION: Do *not* stage any kind of scene that might frighten students or that might be misconstrued in any way when students talk about the event at home.)

There was excitement in Room 45 last week. All the boys were working on a jigsaw puzzle, while the girls were playing with the pet mice. Suddenly, Ralph, a little gray mouse, darted quickly out of Jessica's open hand. It ran as fast as lightning across the room and over Joaquin's foot. Joaquin screamed and started waving his arms around. All at once the puzzle pieces went flying up in the air, then pouring down like a rainstorm. Everyone was screaming.

Writing Tip #22

In a narrative essay, elaborate by writing a whole paragraph that describes a character's thoughts.

One reason we love to read books is because we can tell what the characters are thinking in different situations. We get to know the person as she reflects on scenes from childhood, hatches plans, sees humor in different situations, and bares her soul to the reader in every emotional state. We come to care about the characters the writer has created.

It is vital, therefore, that we teach students how to write what the characters are thinking. This is an activity that you will need to work on with students all year long. But the rewards are great—more fulfilling and complete essays, higher writing assessment scores, and possibly a glimpse into the soul of your young authors.

Hand out copies of the homework sheet (page 73). Before you send this assignment home, do the classroom activity more than once and try to get at different emotions each time—joyful, anxious, scared, carefree. On students' first try, serve as the scribe for the whole-group activity. Later, have students work in small groups to write a paragraph about the character's thoughts. Finally, encourage students to work independently to create a three-sentence paragraph describing their character's thoughts.

"We did this in class" sample answers:

She thinks she may have given the wrong spelling test! What can she do now? Should she apologize to her students? Record the grades anyway? What will the kids think? What will the parents think? Maybe she should just toss out these pages. Maybe the kids and parents won't miss them. Maybe she can just leave that part of her grade book blank. She wonders if anyone would ever know.

In an expository essay, elaborate by writing a whole paragraph that provides a specific example.

The previous lessons all focused on narrative essays, in which students write a personal story, whether it be fiction or nonfiction. These next two lessons focus on creating elaboration paragraphs for expository essays, which explain or give information. Remember that although these are usually nonfiction, they can also be "tongue in cheek" or even blatant fiction. For example, at a writing assessment test in Florida one year, students had to respond to a prompt that asked them to suggest an ideal classroom pet. One student wrote that a brontosaurus would be the prefect pet. The children could feed it the vegetables they didn't want for lunch, and it could stand outside the classroom second-floor window, and kids could slide down its neck to get to the playground. Cute? Absolutely! Did his essay get a high score? How could a scorer resist?

This lesson provides students with some basic transition phrases that will help them include concrete examples to bolster their points in the essay. Be careful not to dwell on transition phrases too much. Some writing programs insist that every paragraph have a transition, resulting in stilted, uncomfortable reading. Transition phrases should flow naturally, so the movement between ideas is seamless.

Avoid teaching students contrived transitions, such as "On the other hand," "Consequently," and "Last, but not least." Rarely can beginning writers use these correctly, and they end up detracting from the quality of the writing. Instead, encourage students to create whole paragraphs that start with these tried-and-true transitions: "My favorite," "The best," "For example," and "For instance."

Hand out copies of the homework sheet (page 75). Be sure to complete the in-class writing activity as a whole-group activity. Later, you may want to let students work in small groups to write the paragraph about a good friend.

"We did this in class" sample answers:

My favorite activity was when Mrs. Lewis let us finger paint in kindergarten. She made everyone put on paint shirts, and she covered our tables with plastic wrap. Then she spread out the brown finger paint. We made all kinds of smears and pictures. When I licked my finger, I realized that it wasn't paint at all. It was chocolate pudding! What a great surprise!

For example, when I lost my spelling list I went into a panic. I knew the test was the next day, and my parents were already upset about my bad spelling grades. I called Marco, and he read the words to me over the phone. He saved me from a bad grade in spelling.

In an expository essay, elaborate by writing a whole paragraph that provides a short vignette.

In most expository essays, a writer makes his or her main points and then follows up with explanations. These explanations support the topic sentence, so they are called supporting details. To further illustrate a point, the writer might add a vignette—a short, descriptive story—preceded by a transition phrase.

While there are many transition phrases writers could use, keep it simple for students by providing them with just these to get started: "One time," "I remember," "Last summer (or week, year, summer, and so on)," or "When I was." Eventually, students will come up with more transitions of their own. Hand out copies of the homework sheet (page 77).

"We did this in class" sample answers:

I remember one day when I was playing tetherball against Sam. Sam is the tetherball king, and I knew I couldn't possibly beat him. Just as he was about to beat me, his dad called to him from across the playground. As he turned to wave to his dad, I slammed the ball so high he couldn't reach it. I had beaten the king!

Last week I made a mini-pizza with an English muffin, some tomato sauce, and mozzarella cheese. Then I decided to make a face on my pizza. I used two black olives for eyes, a mushroom for the nose, and a slice of green pepper for the mouth. It was fun to make and eat!

Dear Families,

Tonight's homework focuses on narrative essays, which tell a story. Most state assessments require students to write a personal narrative, in which they are the main character, or a fictional narrative, which is about someone else.

The basic five-paragraph format (introduction, three body paragraphs, closing) is a good place for your child to begin writing, but he or she could definitely write much more. As students gain competency in writing, they can start elaborating to make their pieces richer and more interesting to read.

One way to make a story really interesting is to include description. This means more than just adding an occasional adjective here and there. A true description should be an entire separate paragraph. We often tell students to "push the pause button on the video" that is running in their head and write a whole paragraph describing what they see. Read the paragraph below to see how your child described physical characteristics of a person or an animal.

Your Child's Teacher, _____

In a narrative essay, elaborate by writing a whole paragraph that describes the physical characteristics of someone or something in the story.

We did this in class!

Directions: Choose a character from a story you have read this year. Describe that character from head to toe.

❋ **I choose to describe** _____

_____

_____

_____

_____

_____

_____

_____

_____

_____

_____

Families, please help!

Directions: Practice this easy way of writing descriptions of physical characteristics: Describe people from head to toe and animals from nose to tail.

Choose any person you know and describe that person, starting at the top of the head and working your way down to the feet. You can be humorous, but not hurtful. (NOTE: This person can be real or fictional.)

✳ **I choose to describe** _____

_____

_____

_____

_____

_____

_____

Do you have pet at home? Or maybe know of an animal that lives outdoors, such as an ant or a lizard? Take a good look at the animal—real or fictional—and then describe it, starting at the nose and continuing down to the tail. Include details that will make your description interesting to read.

✳ **I choose to describe** _____

_____

_____

_____

_____

_____

_____

✳ **This assignment is due at school on** _____.

_____   _____

Child's name   Parent's signature

Week-by-Week Homework for Building Writing Skills © 2009 by Mary Rose, Scholastic Inc.

VIM8083611
257

Dispatch Note

* A B 1 1 2 0 7 7 5 6 1 5 *

Order Number AB1120775615

Supplied by ABE_US

Catalogue Number **Title and Artist** Qty

= 9780545064071 Week-by-Week Homework for Building Writing Skills 1

9780545135757 Instant Homework Packets Shipped Separately 1

9780545064064 Week-by-Week Homework for Building Grammar, Usage, Shipped Separately 1

Thanks for shopping with us. Please note that if you ordered more than one item we may ship them in separate packets. If you have a query about your order please email us at:

Returns: Please enclose this slip with your items and return to the address on the front of the packet.

Why are you returning the item? _____

Would you prefer a refund or a replacement? _____

Please note, with some items a replacement is not possible.

Dear Families,

Tonight's homework focuses on narrative essays, which tell a story. Most state assessments require students to write a personal narrative, in which they are the main character, or a fictional narrative, which is about someone else.

The basic five-paragraph format (introduction, three body paragraphs, closing) is a good place for your child to begin writing, but he or she could definitely write much more. As students gain competency in writing, they can start elaborating to make their pieces richer and more interesting to read.

One way to make a story really interesting is to describe a scene in detail. In tonight's homework, your child will describe two different scenes—a room and an outdoor view. Have your child simply start in one spot and go around the room or across the scene. This ensures a complete description that truly enhances the quality of the story.

Writing Tip # 20

In a narrative essay, elaborate by writing a whole paragraph that describes a scene or a room.

Your Child's Teacher, _____

We did this in class!

Directions: Write a description of our classroom. Start at the classroom door and look to the left. Describe what you see as you look around the room and back to the doorway.

When we enter the classroom, _____

_____

_____

_____

_____

_____

_____

_____

_____

_____

_____

_____

_____

_____

Families, please help!

Directions: Choose a room in your house. Start at one spot and describe what you see as your eyes move around the room and back to where you are standing. Remember that you are writing a descriptive paragraph, so don't just make a list of what you see. Talk about colors, sizes, and shapes. Your paragraph will be even more interesting if you include sounds, smells, and even tastes.

❋ **I choose to describe** _____

_____

_____

_____

_____

_____

_____

Choose a scene you can actually look at or one you know well, such as your backyard or a neighborhood park. Write a paragraph describing what you see, starting at one place and sweeping your eyes across the scene. Do not simply make a list of what you see.

❋ **I choose to describe** _____

_____

_____

_____

_____

_____

_____

❋ **This assignment is due at school on** _____.

_____   _____
        Child's name   Parent's signature

          Week-by-Week Homework for Building Writing Skills © 2009 by Mary Rose, Scholastic Inc.

Dear Families,

Tonight's homework focuses on narrative essays, which tell a story. Most state assessments require students to write a personal narrative, in which they are the main character, or a fictional narrative, which is about someone else.

The basic five-paragraph format (introduction, three body paragraphs, closing) is a good place for your child to begin writing, but he or she could definitely write much more. As students gain competency in writing, they can start elaborating to make their pieces richer and more interesting to read.

Most students love to write about action in their stories. In tonight's homework, your child will focus on one scene in his or her story and describe everything that happened in detail. This paragraph should be real description and not just a list of what happened. Keep in mind that this is not meant to be the whole story, but just one small paragraph of action within a much longer story.

Your Child's Teacher, _____

In a narrative essay, elaborate by writing a whole paragraph that describes the action.

We did this in class!

Directions: Choose an action that happened at school today or yesterday. Work together to write a paragraph that describes the action. Here are some hints to help you.

❋ Write an opening sentence that tells where the action happened.

_____

❋ Tell the names of the people involved. (You can say "the whole class" or "all of the boys" if you don't want to list everyone's names).

_____

_____

❋ Write the action paragraph. Remember that this is just one action paragraph within a longer story. Include adverbs to help set the mood of the paragraph.

_____

_____

_____

_____

_____

Families, please help!

Directions: Choose a topic from the list below or come up with your own idea for an action paragraph. Then write at least three sentences describing one scene of action. Here are some hints:

- Try to include a simile. This is a comparison using *like* or *as*. For example, "Her eyes sparkled like stars."

- Include adverbs—words that describe verbs, or action words. In the sentence, "He ran slowly," *ran* is the verb and *slowly* is the adverb. It tells how he ran.

- Include adjectives—words that describe nouns. In the phrase, "the red apple," *red* is the adjective for the noun *apple*.

- Describe some real action in your paragraph.

Suggested topics:

- Something funny – perhaps a trick that was done by a family member or a pet
- Something dangerous – maybe a stunt that you saw on television
- Something friendly – think about a thoughtful gesture that one of your friends did
- Something sporty – perhaps a game at school or a sports event

_____

_____

_____

_____

_____

_____

_____

_____

_____

This assignment is due at school on _____ .

_____   _____

Child's name   Parent's signature

Dear Families,

Tonight's homework focuses on narrative essays, which tell a story. Most state assessments require students to write a personal narrative, in which they are the main character, or a fictional narrative, which is about someone else.

The basic five-paragraph format (introduction, three body paragraphs, closing) is a good place for your child to begin writing, but he or she could definitely write much more. As students gain competency in writing, they can start elaborating to make their pieces richer and more interesting to read.

Have you ever read a book and then felt disappointment when you saw its movie version? Perhaps one reason we feel this way is because in movies we cannot tell what the character is thinking. The best actors convey the thoughts of their characters through their actions and facial expressions, but this is rarely as good as reading a character's thoughts as penned by the author. The following lesson will help your child practice writing what characters are thinking—a valuable skill for all writers.

Your Child's Teacher, _____

In a narrative essay, elaborate by writing a whole paragraph that describes a character's thoughts.

We did this in class!

Directions: Read the scene below carefully. Think about what the character might think about the situation in which she finds herself. Then write at least three sentences that tell what she is thinking.

The teacher is at her desk grading papers from a spelling test. She realizes that every student in the class has received a failing grade. She sighs. She frowns. She thinks

_____

_____

_____

_____

_____

_____

_____

_____

_____

_____

_____

Families, please help!

Directions: Read each scene carefully and try to put yourself in the character's situation. Write at least three sentences to tell what that person is thinking. Note: You are welcome to change the last sentence in the prompt if it will help your writing.

It's picture day, but Lisa had forgotten all about it. She is wearing her oldest, shabbiest clothes, and her hair is a mess. When her turn comes for her photograph, she thinks,

_____

_____

_____

_____

_____

You are at a beautiful summer camp. Everywhere you look, you see trees, cabins, and lots of friends. You finally get to choose your activities for the day. You choose archery and think,

_____

_____

_____

_____

_____

Joe is on the school bus, sitting all alone. All the other seats have at least two kids in them. Suddenly the school bully boards the bus and looks around. Joe thinks,

_____

_____

_____

_____

_____

❋ This assignment is due at school on _____ .

_____   _____

Child's name   Parent's signature

Dear Families,

Tonight's homework deals with expository essays. This type of essay informs readers, usually by giving reasons for something. Most state assessments require students to write to a prompt, such as "Who is a person you admire, and why do you admire that person?"

The basic five-paragraph format (introduction, three body paragraphs, closing) is a good place for your child to begin writing, but it is not enough. To get a high score in the state assessment test and demonstrate real writing competency, students should include an elaboration paragraph that gives specific examples. We can help students with this task by providing them with paragraph starters suitable for expository essays, such as, "For example," "For instance," "My favorite," or "The best." See the essay your child wrote below.

Your Child's Teacher, _____

In an expository essay, elaborate by writing a whole paragraph that provides a specific example.

We did this in class!

Directions: Read this essay about why a school is special. Then use the "paragraph starters" to write elaboration paragraphs. Unless you actually attend Middleport Elementary School, this will have to be fiction.

Middleport Elementary School is the best school in the county! We have all the greatest teachers and the best kids.

One reason Middleport Elementary School is so good is the wonderful teachers. They are pretty smart, they don't give lots of homework, and they care a lot about kids. Best of all, they make learning fun with great classroom activities.

My favorite activity was _____

_____

_____

_____

_____

Another reason I love Middleport is that we have the best kids around. I should know because these kids are my best friends. I can always count on my friends if I ever need anything.

For example, _____

_____

_____

_____

_____

I am so glad that I get to come to this school every day. Excellent teachers and helpful friends—what more could a kid ask for?

Families, please help!

Directions: Read this essay about why Friday is a favorite day of the week. Then use the "paragraph starters" to write elaboration paragraphs. These can be true or fictional, so have fun with your assignment.

TGIF! I used to hear that and not understand what it meant. Now I know that it means: "Thank Goodness It's Friday!" And I agree. Friday is my favorite day of the week for two reasons, and this essay will explain them both.

I love Friday because it is always pizza night at our house. My dad says that all of the restaurants are too crowded on Fridays, so I can always count on staying at home for supper. My mom loves having pizza too because she doesn't have to cook.

The best pizza is _____

_____

_____

_____

_____

Another reason Friday is great is that there is no school the next day. That means having friends over for sleepovers and playing board games. My friends and I can also stay up late and watch all kinds of movies.

My favorite movie is _____

_____

_____

_____

_____

It is only three more days until Friday. I can't wait! I still say it is the best day of the week because my family and friends have a great time on Fridays. TGIF!

✳ **This assignment is due at school on** _____ .

_____   _____
          Child's name   Parent's signature

Week-by-Week Homework for Building Writing Skills © 2009 by Mary Rose, Scholastic Inc.

Dear Families,

Tonight's homework deals with expository essays. This type of essay informs readers, usually by giving reasons for something. Most state assessments require students to write to a prompt, such as "Who is a person you admire, and why do you admire that person?"

The basic five-paragraph format (introduction, three body paragraphs, closing) is a good place for your child to begin writing, but it is not enough. To get a high score in the state assessment test and demonstrate real writing competency, students should include an elaboration paragraph that features a vignette—a short, descriptive story. We can help students with this task by providing them with paragraph starters such as, "I remember," "One time," or "Last week (or month, year, summer, and so on)."

Your Child's Teacher, _____

Writing Tip #24

In an expository essay, elaborate by writing a whole paragraph that provides a short vignette.

We did this in class!

Directions: Read this essay about what a child likes to do after school. Then use the "paragraph starters" to write elaboration paragraphs that feature very short stories.

Class dismissed! Those are sweet words to me. Don't get me wrong. I like school and I like my teachers, but I am also glad when school is out. It means that I am on my way to my favorite two activities.

I go to day care after school, but it is pretty cool. We go to a big playground and run around like crazy. Then, after we run around a little, we get to play games. I like tetherball and four-square.

I remember one day when I was playing tetherball _____

_____

_____

_____

We also have snacks at day care. They make us eat healthy stuff, but it is sort of fun because we get to fix it ourselves. It gets a little messy, but they don't even yell at us.

Last week I made _____

_____

_____

_____

Okay, so it isn't ice-skating or karate lessons, but it is a good place to go after school. I am glad I get to go to my day care instead of somewhere else.

Families, please help!

Directions: Read the following essay about a favorite place. Then use "paragraph starters" to write elaboration paragraphs that feature very short stories. Your elaborations can be fictional.

"Over the river and through the woods, to Grandmother's house we go!" Have you ever heard that song? It is usually played at Thanksgiving, but I sing it every time I am going to my favorite place—my grandparents' home.

The main reason I love to visit my grandparents is because they have so much time for me. My parents work all the time, but my grandparents are retired and look forward to having me visit. My grandfather always takes me fishing. He taught me how to bait the hook and cast.

One time we went fishing and _____

_____

_____

_____

_____

The other reason my grandparents' house is my favorite place is because it is out in the country. They don't live on a farm or anything, but it is so quiet out there that you can hear all the birds and crickets. You can see lots of stars out there, too. I always feel safe and comfortable in their house.

Last summer when I went to visit _____

_____

_____

_____

_____

My grandparents' home is my favorite place for many reasons. I always love going over the river and through the woods to get there—even if we go in our mini-van on the interstate!

❋ **This assignment is due at school on** _____ .

_____   _____
              Child's name   Parent's signature

Week-by-Week Homework for Building Writing Skills © 2009 by Mary Rose, Scholastic Inc.

Section 4

Figurative Language—Icing on the Cake

Dear Teachers,

This final section will help students put the "icing on the cake." They will be world-famous for their fictional writing. Their pencils will whine from overuse. Papers will pop with paragraphs. Students will be stars when they write as fast as the wind.

Does this paragraph sound funny to you? That may be because it is packed with figurative language. "Icing on the cake" is an idiom; being "world-famous" is hyperbole; "whining pencils" is an example of personification; "papers will pop with paragraphs" is an example of alliteration; students as "stars" is a metaphor; and writing "as fast as the wind" is a simile.

There are eight types of figurative language commonly used by students: simile, hyperbole, alliteration, metaphor, personification, onomatopoeia, paradox, and idiom. My own students remember these with the acronym SHAMPOPI. The six lessons in this section feature the most kid-friendly kinds of figurative language. They can be used any time of the year and may be combined with other writing lessons. Please do not send these lessons home until you have taught these concepts more than once. I do not recommend teaching a lesson on similes and assigning the corresponding homework sheet that very night. If students have difficulty understanding the concept, there will be wailing and gnashing of teeth at the homework table that night. Remember that homework should be practice for skills students already have.

Please note that the final lesson is not about figurative language. Instead, it teaches a short lesson on writing from different points of view—an important skill required in many state standards. Enjoy!

Mary

✳ **Writing Tip #25**

Develop your own voice through the use of figurative language: simile.

For a tasty way to introduce similes to your class, bring in some sort of treat, such as Hershey Kisses®. Tell students that you would gladly share the treat to anyone who can finish the following sentence:

My Hershey Kiss is like a _____.

As students call out words that can go in the blank, write them on chart paper. Each time they come up with a word that actually makes sense, they can have a Kiss. If you notice some students dominating the activity, consider having the class work as a group so that everyone gets a treat eventually. Sample answers might include: *like a raindrop; like a chocolate volcano; like a teardrop; like a giant chocolate chip.*

Next, tell students they could have a second Kiss if they can finish the following sentence:

My Hershey Kiss is as _____ as _____.

On chart paper, write each phrase students volunteer. Sample answers might include: *as sweet as sugar; as hard as a rock; as dark as night; as pointy as a pencil.*

Then, pointing to each chart, announce to students that they have just learned how to write a simile. Explain that they are using a simile any time they make a comparison using *like* or *as_____ as _____.*

Extend this activity by having students cut a Hershey Kiss shape out of aluminum foil or heavy silver wrapping paper. To make it look realistic, have students crumple the foil and then smooth it out again. Next, pass out strips of white paper and ask students to use pale-blue crayons or markers to write a sentence that contains a simile on each strip. This white strip becomes the little paper that sticks out of a Kiss. Display the completed paper Kisses on a "Simile" bulletin board to help students remember to use simile in their writing. Hand out copies of the homework sheet (page 85) and complete the activity as a class.

"We did this in class" sample answers:

1. The room is as hot as the sun.

2. My fingers are as cold as icicles.

3. He ran like a cheetah to get home.

4. He laughed like a hyena.

5. His nose was as red as a cherry.

6. He was as angry as a wet hen.

7. She is as stubborn as a mule.

8. He yelled like a screeching monkey.

Writing Tip #26

Develop your own voice through the use of figurative language: metaphor.

The metaphor is one of the least-understood forms of figurative language. A metaphor is another type of comparison in which we compare two things that are obviously not related. For example, in the sentence "That dog is a bulldozer, knocking down everyone in his path," we know that a dog is definitely not a bulldozer. Unlike a simile, a metaphor makes a comparison without using the words *like* or *as*.

Encourage students to look for metaphors in their readings. Consider creating a chart where students can list metaphors they find. Guide them to notice that the most interesting metaphors are those that use more than one word to describe the thing that is being compared. Hand out copies of the homework sheet (page 87).

"We did this in class" sample answers:

1. The huge dictionary is **a brick that's way too heavy**.

2. The cafeteria is **a jungle filled with hungry monkeys**.

3. The pepperoni pizza is **a sun dotted with red spots**.

4. Jose is so stubborn, he is **a wall that refuses to budge**.

5. My grandmother's cookies are **snowflakes that melt in your mouth**.

6. That tiny kitten is **a tiger ready to pounce**.

7. Lisa's new bicycle is **a shiny race car zooming down the street**.

8. The Internet is **a library filled with endless information**.

Writing Tip #27

Develop your own voice through the use of figurative language: hyperbole and alliteration.

Both children and adults use hyperbole all the time. We are often "too tired to move" or "too hot to breathe," yet we are still moving and breathing. These examples of extreme exaggeration are called *hyperbole*. Please teach your students the proper pronunciation of this word: "hy-PER-bo-lee" (*not* "HY-per-bowl," as most kids tend to say). Guide students to recognize hyperbole when they are reading and to use it when they are writing. Tell them, however, that this is one of those types of figurative language that should be used sparingly.

Another type of figurative language is *alliteration*, in which many words begin with the same letter. Anyone who has ever tried tongue twisters, like "She sells seashells by the seashore," knows about alliteration, even though he or she may not know the term. Alliteration is often used in advertising (Coca Cola, Peter Pan Peanut Butter) or in books and rhymes ("Three Billy Goats Gruff" or "Sing a Song of Sixpence"). These are good starting places to introduce and teach this kind of figurative language.

The homework activity (page 89) asks students to write sentences containing hyperbole and alliteration. As a reminder, please do not use this homework page as a teaching tool. These skills should be well taught before the assignment goes home. They should serve as a review for concepts students have already learned. The answers will, of course, vary greatly, but below are some examples just in case *you* are at a loss for words!

"We did this in class" sample answers:

1. Zac Efron is the best dancer in the world!

2. My toes just froze off and dropped to the bottom of the pool!

3. I knew she would pick me! I am the smartest kid in the universe!

4. Paul plays with his peanut butter and pudding.

5. Micah meandered across the room munching a mozzarella stick.

6. Jennifer just jettisoned the jelly from her jazzy jersey.

Writing Tip #28

Develop your own voice through the use of figurative language: personification.

Personification entails giving human qualities to things that are not human. Writers often do this to set the tone or mood of their writing. Writing that a car "roars to life" sets a different tone than writing a car "creaked and groaned" before starting. To create personification, use vivid and unusual verbs to show the action that the inanimate object makes. Adding adverbs will improve the quality of the writing. Hand out copies of the homework sheet (page 91).

"We did this in class" sample answers:

1. The rusted hinges on the barn door groaned as the storm wind blew.

2. A gentle spring breeze danced around the children on the playground.

3. The refrigerator sighed as the door was opened for the hundredth time that day.

4. The baseball screamed as it sailed into the night sky.

5. The puppy danced when it saw the boy coming home.

Writing Tip #29

Develop your own voice through the use of figurative language: idiom.

An *idiom* is a phrase or expression with a hidden meaning. The meaning of the words taken together has little or nothing to do with the literal meaning of the words taken one by one. Consider, for example, the common idiom "it's raining cats and dogs." Of course, this simply means that it is raining hard. It has nothing to do with either cats or dogs.

Hand out copies of the homework sheet (page 93). Idioms are particularly difficult for people who are new to the English language. Can you imagine if they literally translate the above idiom? Are there animals falling from the sky? If you know of parents who will have difficulty with this assignment, consider providing the student with an alternative worksheet, allowing an ELL to work with another child, or, better yet, pairing the ELL parent with an English-speaking parent who can explain these quirks in our language.

"We did this in class" answers:

1. D; 2. A; 3. F; 4. E; 5. B; 6. C

Homework answers:

1. I; 2. D; 3. G; 4. A; 5. B; 6. J; 7. K; 8. E; 9. H; 10 and 11. C; 12. F

Writing Tip #30

Write from different points of view.

Point of view is not a type of figurative language, but it is a concept students are required to know and part of the language arts standards in several states. Some states (like Florida, where I live) require students to write both expository and narrative essays in the fourth grade, then expository and persuasive essays in the eighth and tenth grades. "Narrative essay" generally means personal, or first-person, narratives. This means that the piece is written from the writer's point of view. When a child is writing about a time her family went on vacation, she would say "I," "we," and "my family" went on a trip. This is first-person writing.

Hand out copies of the homework sheet (page 95). In this activity, students will write in the first person, using "I," "we," and "us." What's the catch? They will pretend to be someone else! For the in-class assignment, students pretend to be a cat and write a first-person narrative about what the cat is doing and thinking. In the homework assignment, they will pretend to be a little boy who receives a new bicycle. Using first-person pronouns, students will write about what happened to him and how he feels about the bicycle.

My name is Collis, and I am a very special cat. I work really hard at trying to sleep at least 20 out of every 24 hours. During the four hours that I am actually awake, I have a lot of work to do. First, I have to entertain my human by playing with those little noisy toys and by flipping the catnip mouse up in the air. She really likes it when I do that little trick. I can tell because it makes her smile.

After I convince my human to feed me, I snuggle beside her on the couch. I am not sure if she likes this or not. She keeps flipping noisy papers around and is constantly writing with a red pen. Sometimes she pets me and I purr, so I guess she likes having me there.

The best part of the day is in the morning when she leaves me alone. She makes up the bed just for me, and I get to sleep all day long in peace.

Dear Families,

Tonight's homework is as easy as pie. You and your child will glide right through this like a knife through butter.

As you might have guessed, the homework is about similes. The first two sentences in this note contain similes. A simile is a comparison using *like* or *as*. It helps the reader know exactly what the author means and often helps "paint a picture" in the reader's mind.

We use similes all the time in our everyday language. You may not even realize that you're using a simile when you say something is as soft as a bunny or as hard as a rock. Help your child write familiar similes like the ones below. Then make up a few of your own!

Your Child's Teacher, _____

Develop your own voice through the use of figurative language: simile.

We did this in class!

Directions: What word do you think should go on these blanks? Fill in the blanks with similes.

1. The room is as hot as _____.

2. My fingers are as cold as _____.

3. He ran like _____ to get home.

4. He laughed like _____.

5. His nose was as red as _____.

6. He was as angry as _____.

7. She is as stubborn as _____.

8. He yelled like _____.

Families, please help!

Directions: Make up your own similes for the following situations. You can't get these wrong unless they absolutely don't make sense, so try to have fun and let your imagination run wild. (HINT: You may choose to finish these with only one word, but many of them will be more effective comparisons if you use several words.)

Similes using *like*:

1. You just hit your thumb with a hammer. It feels like _____.

2. Your little sister cut her own hair. It looks like _____.

3. Your football team has lost every game this season. The players run the ball like

_____.

4. You have the cutest dog in the world. You think he looks like _____.

5. You see a dime on the sidewalk. It is shining like _____.

6. There is something wrong with your parents' car. It sounds like _____.

Similes using *as* _____ *as* _____:

1. You just hit your thumb with a hammer. It is as _____ as _____.

2. Your little sister cut her own hair. It is as _____ as _____.

3. Your football team has lost every game this season. The players are as _____

as _____.

4. You have the cutest dog in the world. He is as _____ as _____.

5. You see a dime on the sidewalk. It is as _____ as _____.

6. There is something wrong with your parents' car. It is as _____ as

_____.

This assignment is due at school on _____.

_____   _____
Child's name   Parent's signature

Dear Families,

Tonight's homework is a piece of cake. Well, not literally, but you probably know what I mean. The first sentence is an example of a metaphor. According to Richard Lederer in *The Play of Words*, "A metaphor is a figure of speech that merges two objects or ideas that are for the most part, different from each other, but turn out to be alike in some significant way." A metaphor differs from a simile in that it doesn't use *like* or *as* to compare things. It just says that something is the other thing.

We use metaphors every day, sometimes without knowing it. For example, you might say to your child, "Your bedroom is a pigsty!" Well, it may be a little messy, but it really still is a bedroom, and since there are no real pigs living there (we hope), it is not exactly a pigsty.

See more examples below and have fun with tonight's homework. It's a blast!

Your Child's Teacher, _____

Develop your own voice through the use of figurative language: metaphor.

We did this in class!

Directions: Finish each sentence by filling in the blank with a metaphor. Remember, a metaphor is when we say something *is* what it obviously *is not*. Try to use more than one word to complete each sentence.

1. The huge dictionary is _____.

2. The cafeteria is _____.

3. The pepperoni pizza is _____.

4. Jose is so stubborn, he is _____.

5. My grandmother's cookies are _____.

6. That tiny kitten is _____.

7. Lisa's new bicycle is _____.

8. The Internet is _____.

Families, please help!

Directions: A metaphor is when we say something *is* what it obviously *is not.* "This homework is a piece of cake" contains a metaphor. The homework is obviously not edible, so these two things—cake and homework—seem to have no connection. Because both the cake and the homework are easy to swallow, the metaphor works. Finish each sentence by filling in the blank with a metaphor. Try to use more than one word to complete each sentence.

1. The flowers in the trees are _____.

2. The last Harry Potter book is _____.

3. The river is _____.

4. The kids in the classroom are _____.

5. This new video game that just came out is _____.

6. This red apple is _____.

7. The snow falling on the ground is _____.

8. The crowded school bus is _____.

9. The goldfish in the bowl is _____.

10. That cloud is _____.

11. The night is _____.

12. My best friend is _____.

✽ **This assignment is due at school on** _____ .

_____   _____
Child's name   Parent's signature

Dear Families,

Have you ever heard someone say, "Those shoes are to die for!"? Well, I doubt any of us are willing to actually *die* for a pair of shoes. This outlandish exaggeration is called hyperbole *(hy-PER-bo-lee)*. Hyperbole can spice up any essay, but it should be used sparingly. We really don't want to read such exaggeration in every paragraph, as its effect is lost if it occurs too often.

Another way to rev up writing is to add alliteration. For example, "Every evening Eugene endeavors to educate himself." Notice all those words that begin with the letter *e*? Alliteration is evident when two or more words start with the same letter or sound. We use alliteration in our daily language—coffee cup, crazy cat, gas guzzler. Just as with hyperbole, we want students to know how to use alliteration, but not in every sentence or paragraph.

Tonight's homework is about writing sentences with hyperbole and alliteration. Feel free to help your child use his or her imagination to be funny and outrageous. Have fun!

Your Child's Teacher, _____

Develop your own voice through the use of figurative language: hyperbole and alliteration.

We did this in class!

Directions: Read each situation below and then complete the accompanying sentence with a hyperbole. Yes, you are expected to write outlandish things. That is the meaning of hyperbole!

Example: You just ran a race across the playground, and you are exhausted. You say, <u>"My legs are going to fall off this very minute!"</u>

1. You just watched *High School Musical*. You say, "_____!"

2. You just jumped into a pool only to discover that the water is freezing cold. You say, "_____ _____!"

3. Your teacher just chose you for "student of the week." You say, "_____ _____!"

Directions: Some students are having lunch together. For each name, write a sentence containing alliteration that uses the beginning letter of the name and that tells about his or her lunch experience. Have fun!

Example: Sid says his salami sandwich smells better than Sally's soup.

4. Paul _____.

5. Micah _____.

6. Jennifer _____.

Families, please help!

Directions: Read each situation below and then complete the accompanying sentence with a hyperbole. Yes, you are expected to write outlandish things. That is the meaning of hyperbole!

Example: You just fell and skinned your knee. You say, "I am bleeding to death!"

1. You just stepped on the cat's tail. You say, "_____!"

2. You are watching a thunderstorm from your window. You say,

"_____!"

3. Your teacher just announced that you won the art contest. You say,

"_____!"

4. Your best friend just told you she is moving out of state. You say,

"_____!"

5. You realize you left your backpack on the school bus. You say,

"_____!"

Directions: Some friends are at the playground together. For each name, write a sentence containing alliteration that uses the beginning letter of the name and that tells about his or her playground experience. Have fun!

Example: Susan slides into the slippery sand.

1. Erika _____.

2. Bill _____.

3. Harry _____.

4. Julia _____.

5. Choose a name here: _____.

※ **This assignment is due at school on** _____.

_____   _____
                  Child's name   Parent's signature

Dear Families,

Does your kitchen table groan under the weight of evening homework? Are the books on your shelf begging to be read? Are the bills screaming to be paid?

Each of these questions contains an example of a type of figurative language known as *personification*. When writers use personification, they give human characteristics to animals or inanimate objects. I could probably stand in your kitchen for an hour and not hear any groaning, begging, or screaming, at least not from the table, the books, or the bills.

In tonight's homework, your child should add appropriate action words (verbs) to complete each sentence. Then he or she will write sentences containing an example of personification. Have fun and let your imaginations run wild!

Your Child's Teacher, _____

Develop your own voice through the use of figurative language: personification.

We did this in class!

Directions: Fill each blank with a word that will give the topic of the sentence a human characteristic. (HINT: You may need to add more than one word to complete the thought.)

Example: The moon <u>smiled</u> down on the children in Halloween costumes.

1. The rusted hinges on the barn door _____ as the storm wind blew.

2. A gentle spring breeze _____ the children on the playground.

3. The refrigerator _____ as the door was opened for the hundredth time that day.

4. The baseball _____ as it sailed into the night sky.

CHALLENGE: Animals are slightly more difficult to personify.

5. The puppy _____ when it saw the boy coming home.
   (In this sentence, you can't say "barked," "yipped," or "jumped up," because a puppy would bark or yip or jump. What would a human do when he sees the child coming home?)

Families, please help!

Directions: Fill each blank with a word that will give the topic of the sentence a human characteristic. (HINT: You may need to add more than one word to complete the thought.)

Example: The computer <u>refused to run</u> all morning long.

1. The telephone _____ for the seventh time.

2. The stool _____ under the weight of the elephant.

3. The flowers _____ in the summer sun.

4. The bulldozer _____ to life.

5. The sun _____.

6. The bird _____.

7. The wind _____.

8. The pencil _____.

9. The flag _____.

10. The shoes _____.

Write five sentences that contain personification. You can follow the form of the sentences above.

11. _____.

12. _____.

13. _____.

14. _____.

15. _____.

✳ **This assignment is due at school on** _____ .

_____   _____
Child's name   Parent's signature

Dear Families,

Does the word *idiom* ring a bell? I am not pulling your leg. Just keep your fingers crossed that your child can remember what *idiom* means.

Did you recognize the three idioms in the above paragraph? An idiom is an expression that means something special to us in our language, but would make no sense at all if you looked at the words one by one. For example, if someone is "the top banana," it doesn't mean that the person is a banana. This expression indicates that someone is important.

Tonight's homework asks children to match idioms with their meanings. If you are new to English, you may have difficulty with this assignment and may need to ask a friend to help. If you really have no idea what these idioms mean, please contact me so that I can provide an alternative assignment for your child.

Your Child's Teacher, _____

P.S. The idioms in the opening paragraph were: "ring a bell," which means something sounds familiar; "pulling your leg," which means teasing; and "keep your fingers crossed," which means hope for good luck.

Writing Tip #29

Develop your own voice through the use of figurative language: idiom.

We did this in class!

Directions: Match the idioms in the left column with their meanings in the right column.

1. Every Harry Potter book <u>sells like hotcakes.</u>	**A.** If you start early, you will be more successful.
2. <u>The early bird catches the worm.</u>	**B.** You will be extremely happy.
3. Biking is <u>as easy as rolling off a log.</u>	**C.** Don't complain about things that cannot be changed.
4. <u>We'll cross that bridge when we come to it.</u>	**D.** Something that sells quickly.
5. You'll be <u>tickled pink.</u>	**E.** Don't worry about future events now.
6. <u>Don't cry over spilled milk.</u>	**F.** It requires very little effort.

Families, please help!

Directions: Match the idioms in the left column with their meanings in the right column. (HINT: There are two idioms with the same meaning. Can you find them?)

1. John sat there <u>like a bump on a log</u>.	**A.** There is something good even in bad situations.
2. Tommy's mother <u>put her foot down</u> and told him to be home by noon.	**B.** There are several ways of reaching the same goal.
3. Mr. Jones <u>ran off at the mouth</u> about having neighborhood kids in his yard.	**C.** Gave away a secret
4. <u>Every cloud has a silver lining.</u>	**D.** To make a firm statement and refuse to change your mind
5. There is <u>more than one way to skin a cat</u>.	**E.** Why aren't you talking?
6. She was <u>as mad as a wet hen</u>.	**F.** Don't risk everything on one idea that might fail
7. You <u>can't have your cake and eat it too</u>.	**G.** To talk too much or talk nonstop
8. Has the <u>cat got your tongue</u>?	**H.** Strong desire for sweet foods
9. I have a terrible <u>sweet tooth</u>.	**I.** To be inactive and not responding
10. He <u>spilled the beans</u>.	**J.** Angry and ready to fight
11. She <u>let the cat out of the bag</u>.	**K.** You can't have both things when you are forced to choose only one.
12. <u>Don't put all of your eggs in one basket</u>.	

✳ **This assignment is due at school on** _____ .

_____   _____
Child's name   Parent's signature

Dear Families,

When a writer creates a story, one of the first things he must decide is from whose point of view to tell the story. Who will do the talking—the thief, the victim, or the policeman? In this homework, your child will pretend to be a different person and tell the story from that perspective. For example, if your child were to tell a story from a pencil's point of view, it might sound like this:

Hey! I'm talking to you, kid! Stop squeezing me so hard! And stop chewing on my middle! What do you think I am? An ear of corn? And please get me sharpened. I can hardly write with this dull point.

In this example, the writer uses first-person pronouns, and it's clear that we are reading the thoughts and words of the pencil.

In the activity below, your child took a story written from a cat owner's point of view and rewrote it from the cat's point of view. Your child used first-person pronouns to let us know the actions and thoughts of the cat. Use this to guide you in helping your child complete tonight's homework.

Your Child's Teacher, _____

Write from different points of view.

○ We did this in class!

Directions: The following passage has been written from the point of view of a cat owner. On a separate sheet of paper, rewrite these paragraphs from the point of view of the cat. (HINT: Tell what he is thinking when he plays with his toys or purrs or gets ready to sleep, and what the cat thinks of "his human.")

A Day in the Life of Collis

My cat, Collis, has a very difficult life. There are 24 hours in a day, and he sleeps about 20 of those hours. That leaves four whole hours of each day when he actually entertains me. He plays with his little rattle toys and throws his catnip mouse up in the air. I love it when he does this because he seems to be smiling.

Every evening I feed him supper. Then he snuggles beside me on the couch as I read the newspaper and grade school papers. He purrs all evening and then follows me to bed. When I get up to go to school every day, I know he stays on that bed the whole time I am gone. It is part of his 20-hour "cat nap."

Families, please help!

Directions: This passage is written from the parent's point of view. Rewrite it from the child's point of view. How did you feel about the bike? What were you thinking of? How did you feel when you got on? What tricks can you do? What did your friends say?

My husband and I knew that this would be the happiest day of our son's life. It was the day he was finally going to get a brand-new two-wheeled bicycle. We shopped for two weeks to pick out the perfect one that we were sure he would like. We probably should have taken him with us, but we wanted this to be a big surprise.

On Sunday afternoon we led him to the garage and pulled the sheet off the shiny new bike. Benjamin just stood there and stared. At first we couldn't be sure if he loved it or hated it. Then he broke into a big grin, jumped on and dashed down the driveway, pedaling as fast as he could. At the end of the street we saw him doing tricks and showing off for his friends. We guess he liked it!

It was the happiest day of my life. _____

_____

_____

_____

_____

_____

_____

_____

_____

_____

_____

✳ **This assignment is due at school on** _____ .

_____   _____
Child's name   Parent's signature

Week-by-Week Homework for Building Writing Skills © 2009 by Mary Rose, Scholastic Inc.